PENGUIN BOOKS
NUMEROLOGY MADE EASY

Anupam V. Kapil is one of the leading numerologists in the country. He completed his Masters degrees in Communications and Journalism, and Business Administration from Pune University.

Anupam Kapil writes a column for the *Times of India*. He is also on the panel of experts of the astrology website of the *Times of India,* indiatimes.com. His areas of specialization include palmistry, gem therapy, vaastu shastra, remedial measures in Vedic astrology and study of the *Lal Kitab*.

Anupam Kapil lives in Pune.

Numerology Made Easy

Anupam V. Kapil

PENGUIN BOOKS

An imprint of Penguin Random House

PENGUIN BOOKS

USA | Canada | UK | Ireland | Australia
New Zealand | India | South Africa | China | Singapore

Penguin Books is part of the Penguin Random House group of companies
whose addresses can be found at global.penguinrandomhouse.com

Published by Penguin Random House India Pvt. Ltd
4th Floor, Capital Tower 1, MG Road,
Gurugram 122 002, Haryana, India

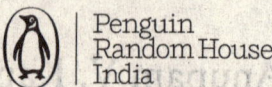

First published by Penguin Books India 2001

Copyright © Anupam V. Kapil 2001

All rights reserved

18 17 16 15 14 13 12

The cover shows the sacred seal of King Solomon which was believed to be
a very powerful charm for evoking spirits when used with the pentacle of
Solomon. It is still used by those interested in magic and psychic matters.

ISBN 9780141004235

Typeset in Sabon by Mantra Virtual Services, New Delhi

Printed at Manipal Technologies Limited, India

This book is sold subject to the condition that it shall not, by way of trade
or otherwise, be lent, resold, hired out, or otherwise circulated without the
publisher's prior consent in any form of binding or cover other than that in
which it is published and without a similar condition including this condition
being imposed on the subsequent purchaser.

www.penguin.co.in

MIX
Paper | Supporting
responsible forestry
FSC® C043100

This is a legitimate digitally printed version of the book and therefore might not
have certain extra finishing on the cover.

*Dedicated to my dear father Vijyendranath Kapil,
without whose support and encouragement this work
would not have been possible.*

Contents

Acknowledgements

I would like to thank Aslesh Laxminarayan, Chandraswami, P.C. Sorcar and R.K. Baquaya for their help and encouragement, and the *Times of India* for their immense support at all times.

I express my gratitude to Lord Shri Ganesh and Ma Vaishnodevi for their blessings.

All About Numbers

What is Numerology?

Numerology is the science of numbers used to determine the trend of your life and predict your future. The two things you need to work out your numerological chart are your date of birth and your full name.

In numerology, there is a number value assigned to each letter of the alphabet. Language and numbers are our means of communicating thoughts and concepts, and the two bear a close relationship to each other. The vibrations you emit and attract are determined by the numerical values of the letters in your name.

When your name is converted into numbers, its relationship with your date of birth determines your talents, your potential, your environment and your relationships.

Numerology indicates the signposts of your life. It helps in understanding yourself and thereby making the best use of the opportunities you encounter. It is a tool to gain insight and knowledge, and to get the best out of your life.

With a few exceptions, numerology deals with single digit numbers, that is 1 to 9. Thus, in almost all cases, after you add up the numerical value of your name or date of birth, you need to add the digits in the total and reduce it to a single digit, the numerological significance of which is listed.

When dealing with letters of the alphabet, each letter has a precise numerological value assigned to it. This can be according to two different systems: the Pythogorean values or the Kabala values. These are explained in the third section of the book.

All numbers have good or bad aspects. Thus their classification as positive and negative is relative. Also, what is important is not the individual number of your chart, but how all the numbers act in conjunction with one another.

In numerology, conventionally when you are making calculations, you use the birth month first, then the birthday and finally the birth year. Thus if your date of birth is 28 November 1968, for calculations it is 11, 28, 1968.

The Evolution of Numerology

Numerology is an ancient science which draws together numbers, letters and astrology. Its development was thus influenced by the development of these three.

All ancient civilizations—the Babylonians, the Hebrews, the Greeks, the Egyptians and the Indians—used numerical systems to decode secret messages in their respective scriptures. The Chaldeans or Babylonians were the first to study the occult sciences deeply and to fix phonetic values to the letters of the alphabet.

The Babylonians (c. 2000 BC) were proficient in astrology and are credited with creating the first recorded astrological system. The Assyrians also made major contribution to astrology.

The Phoenicians learnt the basic concepts of the alphabet from the Hebrews and Egyptians, and developed it to a degree of sophistication and added the vowel sounds around 1000 BC. Earlier Egyptian heiroglyphics existed from 3000 BC. In about 800 BC, the Greeks modified the twenty-two-symbol Phoenician alphabet to form their own, which served as the basis of the Roman alphabet which is need for writing English and other European languages today.

The evolution of numbers is less clear. Cavemen used sticks to mark the sand for counting. About 580 BC, the Greek philosopher Pythagoras founded a university at Crotona for the study of numbers. Pythagoras travelled widely and studied the teachings of the Egyptians,

Assyrians and Indians. He taught that mathematics, music and astronomy formed the triangle of all arts and sciences and were the basis of all knowledge. For practical calculations he used arithmetic, and for spiritual he used numerology. Pythagoras believed that there was nothing that could not be explained by numbers. He, like the ancient Greek philosophers, believed that numbers possessed mysterious powers independent of their arithmetic significance.

Pythagorean numerology formed the spiritual basis for many secret societies, such as the Rosicrusians, the Masons and the Anthrosophists. During the Renaissance, astrology and numerology were taught in the universities and revered as sciences.

In India, certain syllables were considered holy, specially Om which is said to contain the essence of the Vedas.

The Indus Valley Civilization used numbers with precision. Accurately cut cubes in ratios 1:2, 32:64 and 320:640 used as weights have been found during excavations. This system of weights is unique. It is interesting to note that the ratio is based on 16, an important number in ancient Indian numerology. The layout of the cities indicates good knowledge of simple geometry.

The earliest Sanskrit text that deals with astronomy is *Jyotisha Vedanga* (c. 500 BC) which gives the rules for calculating the positions of the new moon and full moon. The *Taittriya Samhita* which speaks about the lunar-solar calendar, probably is even older, from about the seventh century BC.

Early Indian cosmologies are based on the square and the series of numbers 4, 12, 28, 60 obtained as subdivision of the square. Ancient Indian mathematicians developed the system of expressing large numbers in powers of 10, and the division of time into its smallest units. There are references to these powers of numbers in the Vedic *Samhitas, Brahmanas-sutras*, the Mahabharata, and the Ramayana. The *Satapatha Brahmana* refers to the unknown quantity, designated x. *Surya Siddhanta* was written by 400 BC, Varahamihira's *Panchasiddhantika* by 505 AD. Varahamira's other massive contributions to astrology include *Brihatjatika, Brihatsamhita, Laghujatika* and *Romaka Siddhana,* which shows Greek influence. Other scholars whose contributions have helped in the evolution of numerology are Aryabhatta (c. 499 AD), and Brahmagupta and Bhaskara. Parashara's *Horashashtra* (fifth century AD), was the first major numerological treatise. Indian mathematicians brought intuitive insight into the behaviour of numbers, and their arrangement into patterns and series. *Ganita Kaumudi* (c. 1356) by Narayana is notable for its treatment of magic squares.

One of the most important people in the development of numerology in the twentieth century was Count Louis Hamon, popularly known as Chiero. His research into ancient Hebrew and Chaldean systems of numerology and astrology have contributed much to the development of occult sciences. Others who have made significant contributions to numerology in the twentieth century are Sepharial, Helen Hitchcock and Mrs Dow Balliet.

The Occult Symbolism of Numbers

Pythagorus stated that each number has a certain influence which affects all things to which it is related. Thus a digit has not only a quantitative value, it also has a qualitative one.

1 This represents assertion, individuality, manifestation of the finite and unmanifest, the ego, egotism, self-reliance, dignity and ownership. According to Pythagoras, this represents God, infinity, intellect, matter, chaos, void, oblivion, a virgin, the sun, the point within the circle and the fire deity. He favoured this as the father of numbers, and ascribed odd numbers to greater gods, and even numbers terrestrial gods. In its negative aspect this number may represent arrogance, selfishness, and limitation.

2 This number is associated with sensitivity and duality. It denotes creation and production, and is a symbol of the moon. It represents antithesis of good and evil. It is also associated with mourning and death. The occult symbols for this number is the High Priestess. The negative qualities associated with it are excessive criticism, susceptibility to flattery and unreliability.

3 This number symbolizes the trinity (force, matter and consciousness) and the family (father, mother and child). It also represents the past, present, and future. The triad is considered the first perfect number. Every virtue is believed to originate from it. It is also considered the

number of highest wisdom and perfect love. In both Hindu and Christian faiths, the trinity represents the different faces of the godhead.

4 This is the number of the material universe, reason, science and knowledge. The cross and the swastika have four points each. There are four seasons in a year, four sides to a square and four humours. Pythagoreans believed this to be a number of miracles.

5 This number is associated with understanding, justice, the harvest and freedom. It is associated with the five wounds of Christ and the five ancient Chinese elements: earth, fire, water, metal and wood. In Greece and Egypt this number was considered powerful as it was formed by the union of the first odd number and the first even number, and was used as a talisman. In its negative aspects the number may indicate unreliability, black magic and sexual incontinence.

6 This is the number of sympathy, marriage, communion and harmony. It is a symbol of Venus. 666 is supposed to be the emblem of the devil. It was in the sixth hour of the sixth day that temptation came into the world, according to Christian belief. Pythagoreans believe that all things were regenerated after a period of 216 years (the cube of 6). The sixth day was sacred for Druids. It may also indicate anxiety, obstinacy and low self-esteem.

7 This represents completion, immortality, time and space. It is associated with the seven days of the week, the seven ages, the seven planets and seven forces of nature according to Hinduism, and the seven seals. In occult philosophy, it is considered sacred. In Hindu, Christain, Jewish and Buddhist philosophy this the number is related to the godhead. In its negative aspects, this number is

associated with being dictatorial, restless and opinionated.

8 This is the number of dissolution, madness, regeneration and invention. The occult symbol of this number is the figure of justice with a sword and scales. The Greeks regarded this number as one of great power. The negative aspects of this number are introspection and lack of self-confidence.

9 This number represents new birth, spirituality and revelation. When multiplied by any number, the sum of the digits of the product will always add up to 9 (3x9=27; 2+7=9). It has many mystical associations. In Hebrew, this number represents the godhead. Christ is said to have died in the ninth hour. Its negative influences are lack of mercy and compassion.

11 This is a master number in numerology. It indicates new beginnings on a higher plane with inspirational or psychic qualities.

13 This number is traditionally considered unlucky, but it is not always so. In Hebrew tradition, it is a number of change. In the *Sepher Yetzirah*, the thirteenth path signifies understanding of all spiritual knowledge. The unlucky association comes from the Last Supper. There are thirteen Buddhas and thirteen Mexican snake gods. In the Kabala, this number represents the emperor, armed to gain his empire.

22 The significance of this number is derived from the fact that it is the sum of 3 (the Trinity), 7 (the number of planets) and 12 (the signs of the Zodiac). It thus connects the spiritual and the material. It also represents the illuminated intellect and is a master number.

Numerology and Astrology

Astrology and numerology are closely related to each other. The rulership of planets and numbers are linked to the signs of the zodiac.

Sun sign	Dates	Planet	Number
Aries	21 March to 19 April	Mars	9
Taurus	20 April to 20 May	Venus	6
Gemini	21 May to 20 June	Mercury	7
Cancer	21 June to 20 July	Moon	2, 7
Leo	21 July to 20 August	Sun	1, 4
Virgo	21 August to 20 September	Mercury	5
Libra	21 September to 20 October	Venus	6
Scorpio	21 October to 20 November	Mars	9
Sagitarius	21 November to 20 December	Jupiter	3
Capricorn	21 December to 20 January	Saturn	8
Aquarius	21 January to 20 February	Saturn	8
Pisces	21 February to 20 March	Jupiter	3

The days of the week are also associated with specific numbers and planets.

Day	Number	Ruled by
Sunday	1, 4	Sun
Monday	2, 7	Moon and Neptune
Tuesday	9	Mars
Wednesday	5	Mercury
Thursday	3	Jupiter
Friday	6	Venus
Saturday	8	Saturn

What Your Sun Sign Indicates

Aries Impulsiveness and spontaneity are your characteristic features. You are extravagant, forceful and energetic. You are also enthusiastic, ambitious and independent. You have natural leadership qualities.

Taurus You have great powers of retention and are secretive. You are good at finance, practical, and exacting. However, you may also be domineering and stubborn.

Gemini You are of dualistic nature, nervous and restless. But you are also quick and active, with great powers of intellect.

Cancer You are sympathetic and kind. You have an instinct for personal aggrandizement. You are emotional, sensitive and receptive. You desire power and fame.

Leo This sign indicates spirituality and generosity. It is also a sign of power, vitality and organizational ability. The distinguishing characteristics are loyalty and lavishness.

Virgo You are critical and analytical, with a tendency to worry. You are also eloquent, discriminating and wise.

Libra You have a balanced, harmonious personality. You are artistic, affectionate and unassuming, with intuitive powers.

Scorpio You have a strong personality, with perseverance and courage. You may also have pride, ambition and envy. You have remarkable mystical powers and great passion.

Sagittarius You have the mind of a genius. Your activities are directed towards a higher state of existence. You are outspoken and generous. The sign indicates aspiration, devotion, love of sport and travel, and sympathy.

Capricorn You are practical and materialistic, with an inclination for business and politics. You have practical ideals, deep thinking, and cool understanding.

Aquarius This sign indicates great involvement with human nature. You have considerable powers of concentration and the ability to read character well.

Pisces You are emotional, sympathetic and benevolent. But you are inclined to worry and be careless in speech.

Planets, Numbers and the Professions They Govern

Planet	Number	Rules over	Professions
Mercury	5	Communication	Writing, advertising, journalism, media, travel
Venus	6	Relationships	Entertainment, dancing, gambling, decoration, design
Jupiter	3	Finance	Banking, trading, arbitration, philanthropy

Planet	Number	Rules over	Professions
Saturn	8	Industry	Mining, property, mathematics, research
Mars	9	Physical work	Armed forces, hunting, sports, trade unionism, surgery
Uranus	4	Occult	Astrology, engineering, intense research
Nepture	7	Art	The arts, divination, music, travel

Mantras

Mantra, yantra and tantra are closely connected with astrology and numerology. A mantra is a sound which when repeated gives rise to certain psychic energies which can be used to produce material effects. Sound waves have numerical frequencies which distinguish one from the other. Ancient Indians were aware that combinations of certain sound frequencies had the power to dislodge and channelize deeper astral energies.

This belief is common to many ancient civilization. Pythagorus stated that each planet had a distinct sound vibration which combined to form the music of the spheres. This is called ananta shabda or aum in the Vedas, logos in the Bible, and kalma-i-illahi in Islam. When this sound is generated by the human body, it leads to liberation of the spirit.

Your Birthday Number

The birthday number is one of the most important indicators in the numerology chart. The vibration of the day you were born on has an enormous influence on your life. It indicates your talents and abilities, as well as your attitudes towards challenges and opportunities.

While you can change your name for a more numerologically favourable one, you cannot change your birthday. The influence of your birthday is greatest between your twenty-eighth and fifty-sixth birthdays.

Birthdays are classified into three classes called concords, which are used to assess compatibilities with other numbers. If two people belong to the same concord, they will be compatible.

Birthdays which reduce to	Concord	Talents
1, 5 and 7	Water	Creative, intellectual, scientific
2, 4 and 8	Fire	Emotional, business
3, 6 and 9	Air	Artistic, eloquent, good people's person

What Your Birthday Number Indicates

1 You are ambitious, logical, independent, strong willed, and a natural leader. You need to be at the helm of affairs as you dislike interference and restraint. You are practical, and a good counsellor. You begin projects well but do not finish them. Routine frustrates you. You have

excellent business instincts and broad vision, and will achieve success. Guard against being lazy.

You need love and companionship, but are undemonstrative. You also crave praise and sympathy. You can be domineering, obstinate and selfish, and handle emotional matters with reason instead of with feeling.

Professions you are suited for include teaching, marketing, analysis, consultancy, work in human resources, aviation or engineering.

2 You are warm-hearted and affectionate. However, you may be emotional and sensitive, and get easily hurt. You should avoid people with negative attitudes as you are susceptible to depression. You are tactful and cooperative, and work better on your own. You are also imaginative and impractical. You are appreciative of beautiful things and your accommodating nature wins you many friends.

You need love and affection. You are a natural peacemaker, and successful in personal relationships. You enjoy change and travelling, and are skilled in music and art. You are intuitive but liable to underestimate yourself and be exploited. A harmonious and peaceful environment is vital for your peace of mind.

You will be successful as a politician, analyst, statesman, musician, actor or writer.

3 You are frank, cheerful and fun loving, and you make friends easily. You are an inspiring speaker with intellectual interests and vivid imagination.

You function best on mental and intellectual planes. Some form of expression—writing, speaking or acting—is vital for your well-being. You are restless, moody and fear loneliness. You have abundant energy and recuperative powers.

You are suited to occupations that bring you in contact

with people—law, music, medicine, advertising and lecturing. You may one of three kinds: artistic and inclined towards literary pursuits, social and unstable by nature, or emotional and drawn to acting.

4 You are practical and believe in hard work and discipline. You are conservative, methodical and cautious. You are respected for your rational thinking. Your stubborn nature makes it hard for you to reverse a decision or express yourself diplomatically. Any change from routine upsets you.

Although you are persevering and have good organizational capabilities, you should be more open to creative ideas. You are devoted to your family, but are not demonstrative. Once you undertake something, you will always complete it. Your reserved nature may cause you to be misunderstood. You should restrain youself from inflicting your opinions on others.

Professions you are suited for are auditing, architecture, the army or manufacturing.

5 You love change, travel and adventure. You are versatile and intellectual, and savour new experiences. You are highly adaptable and a good speaker, therefore you will do well in public relations and writing. Though you have an analytical mind, you may become overconfident and headstrong.

You should not overindulge in food, alcohol, sex and drugs, and guard against nervous tension. You are popular socially, especially with the opposite sex. You should marry young. You tend to try everything but do not finish projects with the enthusiasm you begin with.

Professions where originality and ingenuity come into play are best for you, such as writing, real estate, insurance, analysis, public relations and communications.

6 You are family-oriented. Family and friends influence your career choices. Although you are emotional you are also reserved. You love nature, and need companionship and love. Your easy-going and adaptable nature makes you popular. You appreciate luxury. You are cheerful but neglect or criticism makes you dejected. You are generous and understanding. You love children although you may not receive much happiness from your own.

You lack financial sense. You work best in collaboration. But you may be stubborn and argumentative. Community affairs interest you. You may have artistic talent which should be nurtured.

You will make a good healer, masseur or doctor. You need to achieve balance in your feelings and actions.

7 You are sensitive and should always follow your hunches. You are secretive, and like to do things alone and complete projects. You are drawn to scientific subjects because you have an analytical mind. The influence of the moon makes you restless and travel widely. You have musical, literary or artistic talent. Avoid gambling.

You should guard against the tendency to be self-centred or stubborn. You are likely to be negative to new propositions. The colour purple protects you. The occult and religious subjects attracts you. Professions you are suited for are science, teaching, music, finance, surgery, interior decoration, poetry and astrology.

8 You are strongly individualistic and generally misunderstood. You have good executive ability and a creative and bold approach to business. This is an excellent birthday for business and financial success, but if your name is not in harmony with the birthday, there will be struggles. There will be many gains if you handle

your assets and investments wisely. Partnerships will not bring gains.

You have leadership qualities and organizational abilities but you can become domineering. Challenging business situations stimulate you. Your inclination is more towards material than spiritual matters. However, if you use power and money for selfish purposes, disaster results.

Your reserves of inner strength and resistance are considerable but you should be more flexible. External circumstances, love affairs, legal problems and deaths may significantly affect your destiny.

You will be successful in corporate law, business, accountancy, engineering (especially software engineering) or music.

9 You have a lot of aggression, whether mental or physical. You have strong will power, great intensity and a dominating personality. Your impulsiveness and quick temper may cause you to behave recklessly. You are fond of travelling. You function on an intellectual and artistic plane. Your humanitarian action can help the masses and give you much satisfaction. But sacrifice and unconditional love may be demanded of you.

You have great charm and easily relate to people from different walks in life. Though you are expressive, you can also be sharp and dramatic. Avoid negative attachments and feelings. You may have peculiar psychic experiences.

Professions you are suited for are the armed forces, artistic, theatrical or literary pursuits, teaching, music, law, advertising and the foreign services.

10 You are a born leader. Fame and fortune may be yours. You are extremely independent and aggressive, and may take the law in your hands. You become very stubborn if you are opposed. You are an idealist to the core and strive to improve your

environment. You should develop your creative talents. Your magnetic personality, dynamism and enthusiasm make you popular in professional and social circles. You have considerable executive ability. Routine activities frustrate you and you need to be busy with something constructive and varied. You may be a jealous and possessive friend.

Professions you are suited for include law, advertising, teaching, aviation, police services and human resources management.

11 Many numerologists call this a master number, which makes you have high aspirations and determination. You are very moody and your desires often fluctuate. You are not interfering, and prefer to inspire people rather than get involved in details. Your external calm is deceptive; you are highly strung, excitable and emotional over trivial matters. Being in the limelight inspires you. You are more suited to being an advisor or working in creative or inspirational fields, rather than in business. You should avoid daydreaming and translate your ideas into practice. You have good intuition and should act on your hunches. You tend towards extremes in love. Yoga and meditation will be beneficial.

Public professions like communication or media which bring you in contact with people are suitable for you. If you curb your restless nature and focus, you will be successful in your aims. Tragedies may occur in your life but these shall only precipitate spiritual understanding. You should guard against secret enemies. Professions you will be successful in are dancing, teaching, the media, music and art.

12 You have a touch of genius and live life to the full. You have great enthusiasm and make the best of any situation. You are brilliant and magnetic with good communication skills. You are a good parent but can be rather severe on your children. Though you are gentle and persuasive by nature, you may dominate others to achieve your goals. The influence of the sun (1) and the moon (2) in your birthday gives you these qualities.

You are drawn to literature and the arts. You may be impatient and nervous. Being intellectually occupied always is vital for your peace of mind. You are a good speaker, but often lack tact. Your quick-witted, imaginative and affectionate nature ensures that you are popular with friends and colleagues. You must guard against depression and scattering energies. You should learn to focus. You may have artistic talent which should be nurtured. You successfully take on responsibility and withstand pressure. However, ego problems should be guarded against.

You will be successful in writing, acting, advertising, health, law, architecture and interior decoration.

13 This is not an unlucky number as is widely believed. You are hard-working, methodical and creative. However, you may be misunderstood. You are ambitious and may be dictatorial and stubborn. You detest feuds and cannot tolerate injustice. Your cautious and disciplined nature can make you successful. But you may feel frustrated and restricted by circumstances.

Professions suitable for you are business, accounting, building, mining and merchandising.

14 You love change, excitement and travel. This birthday acts as a bridge between the physical and spiritual worlds and is a dual number. You may be creative and critical at the same time. Though you seem calm, there is emotional turbulence within which makes you moody. You are adaptable and flexible, but you should be careful of being exploited. When there are no restrictions, you

work well with others. You are restless and easily bored, and may change professions and relationships quickly. Though you are versatile and talented, you cannot concentrate on one thing. However, if you dedicate yourself to anything, you will achieve great success. Women born on this date are advised to marry early.

Luck favours you in gambling and games of chance. This birthday favours friendships, socializing and group activities.

Professions you will be successful in are stockbroking, tourism, mining, writing, trading, and being an ENT specialist.

15 This is a powerful birthdate because it has the influence of the sun (1), Mercury (5) and Venus (6=1+5). A peaceful and harmonious domestic environment is essential for your happiness and health. You gain knowledge by observation rather than study or research. You love languages and the arts. You are intelligent and have good memory. You may have interest in black magic and tantra. You are very sensitive and negatively affected by criticism. You are generous, understanding and demonstrative. You seem very gentle, but harbour strong convictions. Despite your cheerful demeanour, you tend to worry.

You are highly creative and artistic. This birthday is associated with both sinners and saints, and many powerful politicians and orators. You attract opportunities and friends, and have financial success.

Those born on this day are well suited to intellectual and artistic pursuits such as teaching, publishing, the arts and medicine.

16 This is a difficult birthday. You are strongly attracted to towards the philosophical and spiritual, and desire to understand the invisible world.

You should follow your hunches. But this will not be easy as you are also a rationalist who tends to analyse and reason. You have strange dreams, often with prophetic meanings. You have excellent concentration and an analytical mind, and should specialize. Though you like solitary contemplation and meditation, you should not become withdrawn. Though you have talent, you may lack purpose and dedication.

You have difficulty in giving and receiving love. You should pay attention to matters of the heart. You resent interference with your plans. You should avoid brooding and being critical and irritable. Living close to nature benefits you immensely.

Professions you will do well in are science, law, teaching, the arts, commerce, psychology, philosophy and metaphysics.

17 You are very individualistic and intelligent. The influence of the sun (1) and Neptune (7) on this birthday gives rise to contradictory qualities. Sometimes you may be generous to a fault, at other times you are terribly stingy. You desire to acquire deep knowledge. Sound judgment, creativity and ambition ensure that you reach the top in any activity. You dislike interference. You may slip into depression when you are not able to fulfil your own high expectations.

You may become too obsessed with power and judgment, and refuse to delegate work. You can be ruthless and dictatorial in business. Logic and reasoning are important to you, and you may not be spiritually inclined. There maybe a vacuum in your love life or some kind of separation, dissatisfaction or restriction in the relationship. But your drive and ambition will see you rise above problems.

Occupations suitable for you are publishing, theatre and any business connected with the earth, such as oil or mining.

18 You have great determination and perseverance in sticking to something until you succeed. You function primarily on an intellectual plane but your emotional and sensitive nature may make you argumentative. You are a born leader, and organize and inspire others. You have an excellent understanding of people and are highly creative. You will do well in politics and public professions. You must avoid being critical and live positively. A great deal of travelling is indicated.

You have noble and humanitarian goals. You are clear and expressive but may become too dramatic. Your enthusiasm and will power ensure success. You have depth in emotion. You will make an excellent critic or writer. You love music. You should live to the higher vibrations of this number. You may be called upon to handle higher responsibilities. If you live selfishly you may face changes, losses and disappointments.

There is a contradiction as the birthday combines the influences of the sun (1) and Saturn (8) which are not harmonious. As a result, you may face problems of ego and adjustment. You are judicious and often side with the underdog. The higher vibration of this birthday demands sacrifice. You should let go of negative attachments and have a spiritual outlook. You may not have a lasting marriage.

Professions you will be successful in are law, politics, religion, stocks and transport.

19 You are a complicated person. The vibration of this number is powerful as it includes all numbers from 1 to 9. You are very resourceful and versatile, and can succeed in almost any profession. Your fortunes may fluctuate greatly. You are obstinate and find it difficult to cooperate with others. You have to learn to make adjustments.

You are demonstrative and subject to emotional extremes. You may be misunderstood in marriage, or not find complete happiness and become lonely. You should not be impetuous in love affairs. Many born on this birthday achieve glory and fame.

20 The influence of the moon makes you loving and sympathetic. You are very patient, pursuasive and diplomatic. Your tactful nature makes you a good mediator. You appreciate music and the arts. You are more suited working in small groups or for others.

You are devoted to your family. You are deeply emotional and should guard against others taking advantage of you. You are also sensitive and impressionable. You are affectionate but expect reciprocation. You can make people accept your point of view through gentle persuasion. If you are born in April or November, you may have bursts of violent temper and aggression. Beauty, harmony and love are the driving forces in your life. Influential women will help you. Dealings across the seas will be very beneficial.

Professions that you can excel in are acting, writing, politics and analysis.

21 This is powerful birthday as it is influenced by the moon (2), the sun (1) and Jupiter (3). The influence of the moon makes you imaginative and creative, and that of the sun gives you a strong will to succeed. You are extremely versatile and talented. You should focus your energies in specialized fields to achieve power and fame. You are very ambitious and desire to be the centre of attention. You should not scatter your energy because of impatience. You need to cultivate poise and patience as you find it difficult to concentrate on a single activity. You can do well in music or theatre.

Your attractive and cheerful personality makes you popular. You are better as a friend than as a spouse as you are impatient and suspicious. You are appreciative of beauty and colour.

This is a number of creativity and expression. Professions best for you are publishing, acting, advertising and journalism. You may be erratic and emotional, and are inclined to brood and become depressed. But you also have charm, good humour and a generous nature. You are always ready to help friends. This birthday is more fortunate for those born in March, October, November and December. Thursdays and Sundays are good for you.

22 This is a master number, which is why if you are born on this birthday, you must try to have altruistic aspirations and not purely personal ones. Periods of rest and seclusion are necessary for you as you are highly strung. Will power and strong determination help you accomplish whatever you desire. You may be misunderstood, have few trustworthy friends and be brought to grief in relationships.

You should live positively as everything you experience is doubly good or bad. You are intuitive, and should rely on first impressions. You analyse well. Most people born on this birthday have major ups and downs in life, and success is achieved late. You need to learn to compromise but are otherwise more suited to working in large groups. You should avoid being extravagant.

Professions you are suited for are exports, teaching, accountancy, law, mining and in the labour industry.

23 This is a fortunate birthday, due to the presence of the moon (2) and Jupiter (3). You belong to the intellectual world but are also very practical. You are quick-witted and adaptable, with a gift for communication and writing. Your magnetic manner makes you successful with people, especially the opposite sex and with older people. You may overindulge in food, alcohol and sex. As you grow older you may suffer from rheumatism.

This birthday indicates you have at least two sources of income. You love freedom and informality. Your strong spirit of independence gives you a desire for domination. Though you will have an eventful life, you may suddenly decide to give up everything.

Professions you are well suited for are acting, film producing, teaching, medicine, science, writing, publishing, marketing and anything to do with the entertainment industry.

24 You are under the combined influence of the moon (2) and Venus (2+4). This is a birthday associated with great financial success. But you have to give up daydreaming and utilize the practical side of your nature. You should fight worry, fault-finding and jealousy. There is a tendency to fickleness and to shift from one activity to another. You are very responsible, generous and devoted to your family. Companionship and love are very important for you, but you may experience heartbreak or problems in marriage. You have a decided inclination towards art and beauty. Harmony is important for you and you can sacrifice much to maintain important relationships. You are versatile and gifted in the arts, alternative therapies, healing or drama.

You are a good and persuasive speaker. Your personality attracts people. Those of high rank and of the opposite sex will help you. You may marry into a rich family. This birthday is good for speculation. You should try to curb your strong ego. You love luxury and material comforts, and have expensive tastes due to the influence of Venus. You also have lots of energy and a craving to achieve. Missed opportunities or wasted time greatly troubles you.

Professions in which you will be successful are in the arts, finance, jewellery, perfumery, food and beverage industry, boutiques, toys and chemicals.

25 This birthdate combines the influence of the moon (2) and Mercury (5) which both relate to the mind and psyche. You are blessed with good intuition and a prophetic disposition. You must heed hunches. You are very emotional, moody and get easily hurt. But as you try to hide your real feelings, you are often misunderstood. You must make an attempt to share your thoughts with people. Trust is the key to your emotional happiness. You should not neglect the heart while using your mind. You are a perfectionist and set high standards for yourself and others. But you underestimate yourself.

You are capable of investigating and researching subjects deeply. You are a thinker and never rush into decisions without deep thought. However, you may become cynical, aloof and critical. You prefer to work alone and make it a point to finish projects once started. You should avoid the tendency to be lazy, melancholy and vacillating. Living a simple life close to nature will be very good for your health and happiness.

You can succeed in the arts. You will be successful in teaching, accounts, astrology, psychology, metaphysics, painting, detective work, writing, politics and science.

26 This birthday is influenced by the moon (2) and Venus (6) which gives you good business and executive abilities. You are an excellent organizer. Your ambitious and intelligent nature allows you to achieve great success. However, you may start several things simultaneously which you find difficult to complete. You have a tendency to live in the past. You should be optimistic and look to the future. You are diplomatic and tactful, and prefer to do things by gentle persuasion. You have a strong character and can be domineering. Generally, you do not express your feelings.

You are generous and can be depended upon for help in a crisis. You may not have smooth relationships as

Saturn, the ruler of this number, creates discord. Problems or delays in love affairs are indicated. As you will rise fast in your profession you may provoke jealousy.

27 This is the birthday of the born leader. You may be dogmatic in thought and eccentric in behaviour. A special talent in politics, religion, arts and law is indicated. Extensive travelling will broaden your mind. You express yourself well, though you may be too dramatic at times. You may suffer from tension and health problems. You are forceful and determined. You are highly psychic but easily disturbed. You are incapable of working in subordinate positions.

You have dramatic and literary abilities. Science, metaphysics and the occult attract you. You may marry early but the relationship may be disappointing. You must avoid stimulants. You are affectionate but erratic. You do not like accountability and may feel deprived of your due in life from your parents or the community. You need to accept and forget. Sacrifice will be a feature in your life. You need to let go of negative attachments and feelings, and develop a philosophical outlook.

Professions you will be successful in are diplomacy, law, journalism, medicine or stockbroking.

28 You are dominating, strong-willed and idealistic, with considerable leadership qualities. This number combines the cooperative abilities of 2 and the practical and executive quality of 8. You see the other person's viewpoint and have an exceptionally analytical and rational mind. Though you are confident, you need encouragement. The influence of Saturn (8) may bring delays and tragedy into your life, and your loyalty and sincerity may be unrewarded.

You are unconventional and independent, and cannot work in subordinate positions. Your friendships and relationships are also unconventional. Though you love freedom, you will encounter limitations. Interest in the occult is indicated. You are emotional and demonstrative. You have excellent debating skills and are creative. You must avoid being lazy and fickle. Most of your troubles are self-created and caused by the tendency to magnify your problems.

29 This is a very powerful birthday. You are perceptive and spiritual, with keen insight into things, though not necessarily through logic or rational thought. You are drawn to activities which bring you in contact with people. You may be nervous and moody. You need to develop hobbies. You feel you are a child of fate and should surrender to higher laws.

There is potential and fire in your personality, but you need to develop character and judgment which will happen in your thirties. You are difficult to live with and understand as you are erratic and self-willed. A peaceful home is essential for you, but your self-absorption may make you careless of the comforts of others. You are sensitive and easily influenced by your surroundings. You have many admirers. You are capable of great love but you crave social recognition and attention.

You may get hurt easily and become depressed. You have leadership abilities and can be forceful to attain your goals. If your name is in harmony with this date, you will achieve outstanding success. You have excellent negotiating skills and diplomacy. You will achieve much if you do not seek fame and success. You should be satisfied with your achievements as excess ambition can lead to your untimely fall or death. Your liaisons could lead to scandal. Guard against pride. You may possess healing skills, though your own health may not be good.

30 You have similar qualities to those born on the 3rd. Your creative talents are highly developed. You do well in anything that requires use of your hands. You are friendly, affectionate and loving, love socializing and are popular. Though you are energetic and efficient, you must avoid a tendency to be erratic. Any kind of executive position suits you. You dislike manual, routine or confining work.

You may have a dual personality. You should live positively and avoid frittering away your energy. You love freedom and expansion. You will be either fabulously wealthy or totally broke. Your fortunes can fluctuate wildly. You may have enormous drive and enthusiasm, but cannot channelize them.

You are imaginative and will do well in dramatics, writing, teaching, advertising or social work. Though you may be interested in the occult, you should be careful as you are susceptible to its influences. This date is favourable for those in secret services, research, banking, debating or government services.

31 This is a good business birthday. You can have the best of both material and spiritual worlds. You must have patience and carry out your plans relying on intuition. You have an excellent memory and never forget kindness or injury. Your aspirations and expectations are unreasonable, and you may be disappointed. You are hard-working, loyal and determined, and will achieve your goals.

There may be bitter disappointments and frustrations in your love life. Early marriage may benefit you. You should develop interests or hobbies, cultivate friends and learn to express your feelings. Though you are original and honest, you are also stubborn and set in your ways. You possess good organizational and managerial skills with an eye for detail. Your discipline and consistency makes co-workers rely upon you. You should be careful not to overwork and find time to relax. You should cultivate faith and apply yourself to opportunities in hand to find stability in both career and personal life.

Professions you are suited to are medicine, architecture, accountancy, writing and contracting.

Your Fate Number

This is calculated by adding the digits of your birthday and reducing the sum to one digit. Thus if you are born on the 12th, your fate number is 1+2=3.

What Your Fate Number Indicates

1 This is the fate number of those born on the 1st, 10th, 19th and 28th of any month. You are influenced by the sun. The sun is its peak strength when situated in the sign of Aries (21 March to 21 April). Its influence is particularly strong if you are born on a Sunday, especially between 21 July and 21 August as the sun is also the ruling planet of the sign Leo. The sun is weakest when in the sign of Libra (21 September to 21 October). If you are also born in the planetary hour of the sun (see p. 195), the influence of this number is even more powerful.

You are highly individualistic, very ambitious and cannot be restrained by circumstances or people from forging ahead once you have set yourself a goal. A very assertive nature makes you resent any kind of interference or restraint. This, in addition to your love for working alone, may make you dictatorial. You may also become unpopular due to your obstinate nature. As you have strong leadership qualities, you would be well suited to working in big organizations where you can show your talents and rise to the top. Your strong views and convictions enable you to push through your plans and schemes. But you are ready to change your opinions if others suggest good enough reasons to do so. Your reliability and dependability are unquestionable. Your positive attitude helps you to face ups and downs without losing courage. You are always on the lookout for new things and do not follow the beaten track. The ability to take quick decisions, coupled with a far-sighted approach, ensures your success. Professional advancement will start after your twenty-fifth year, and the period between your thirty-fifth year and forty-ninth year will be filled with activity. If you are born in August, you will be lucky in financial matters and have new openings from your thirty-seventh year. 3, 6 or 9 in your date of birth are fortunate for you; 2, 5 and 8 indicate you may be led astray at times.

You will achieve proficiency in specialized fields which may not be your main line of activity. Your desire for freedom makes you unsuitable for subordinate positions. You are very direct in speech and dislike pretence and hypocrisy. You have good manners and fine tastes, and you dislike flattery, false pride and egotism. Though you are generous and helpful by nature, you are in constant need of appreciation and recognition. As you are very creative, you will be successful in work requiring originality. However, if you do not succeed, you become pessimistic and depressed. Strong will power and sound logical and reasoning faculties make you popular with friends and colleagues. Though you seem unapproachable, you readily help those in serious trouble. Your warm and sunny disposition will make you immensely popular with the opposite sex. You will benefit from women. Travels and adventure attract you. You desire to become famous or a leader in whatever you do. As the sun is the ruler of this number, you will receive the support of people in authority. You are fond of gracious living and spend lavishly on those you love.

If 1 is repeated more than twice in your date of birth, you will receive favours from the government. If it is repeated more than three times in the birth date and connected with 3, 6 or 9 you might attain international fame or be an eminent occultist or astrologer. Repetition of the digit twice along with 5 also repeated twice will make you eminent in legal, judicial or educational fields. If you have one or two 0s in the birth date, you must consider deeply before taking major professional decisions.

Precautions: You must avoid being too ambitious, independent, reckless, critical, boastful and wary of asking for help. You must try not to live in a house where the house number adds up to 4 or 8. Try to be more flexible in your approach. Use of copper in any form on your body, prayer room or work table is advisable.

Strong Periods: The best period for you is between 21 March and 28 April and 20 July and 20 August.

Weak Periods: This is when the sun starts losing strength. During October, November and December, you may feel disinterested in work and stressed. Your health may also suffer. Be cautious before starting anything new or making investments.

Good Days: Sunday and Monday are the most fortunate days for you, especially if you are also born on these days.

Good Dates: Dates that vibrate to your number are the 1st, 10th, 19th and 28th of any month. The other series of numbers that is favourable to you is the 2, 4, 7 series, i.e. on the 2nd, 4th, 7th, 11th, 13th, 16th, 20th, 22nd, 25th, 29th or 31st.

Health: You have problems with the circulatory system and should do exercises which help improve circulation. Your temperament is bile dominated, and you should avoid oily foods, meat and fish, and also eat early in the evening.

Relationship with Other Numbers

Fate number 2	Good as friends, but not as spouse
Fate number 3	Good as friends
Fate number 4	Do not marry though this number gives you energy
Fate number 5	Can only be a friend
Fate number 6	Good compatibility due to shared ideals and discipline, good as friends or lovers
Fate number 7	Better as a friend than spouse
Fate number 8	Good as lover, not good as spouse
Fate number 9	Good relationship due to common ambitious nature and perfectionism

Favourable Colours: Orange, yellow, copper and golden are best for you.

2 This is the fate number of those born on the 2nd, 11th, 20th and 29th of any month. You are ruled by the moon which governs the period between 21 June and 21 July. The moon is in its peak strength between 21 April and 21 May and is at its weakest between 21 October and 21 November.

You are gentle, imaginative, artistic and inventive. You function more on the mental plane than the physical. You have a romantic nature and well-developed intuition. Though you are peaceful by nature, you are also restless. Your imaginative nature makes you inventive, but you may lack the determination to execute your ideas. The influence of the moon gives you a love for fragrances. You are stubborn and will not do anything unless you know the reason for the action. You are a devoted lover and regard vows as sacred. You are sensitive and have deep feeling for the difficulties of others.

Many artistically talented people are born under this number. You are a good negotiator and the cause of justice is sacred to you. However, you need to be diplomatic while expressing yourself. This number indicates literary ability. If you have 9 in your date of birth, you will be adaptable and resourceful.

You are always afraid of losing love, friendship, money and property. You are attached to your mother. You are very secretive but good at finding out the secrets of other people. Money will never be a problem for you, and you contribute generously to charitable organizations. You appreciate people who are kind-hearted, gentle and helpful, and friendships are sacred to you.

You should guard against restlessness, lack of self-confidence and ambiguity in your plans. Your strong and demanding nature isolates you. Unhappy surroundings make you despondent. You must learn to overcome fear and possessiveness, and rely on your intuitions to fulfil your dreams. Yoga, meditation and introspection are good means of relaxation for you, as are outdoor sports and activities. Being with nature recharges your batteries. Professions suitable for you are politics, psychology and literary work. You must become more independent. Do not leave jobs unfinished due to loss of interest. Keep away from flatterers and avoid acting in haste.

Strong Periods: The best period for you is 21 June to 21 July.

Weak Periods: During January, February and July, you may face health or psychological problems. Avoid taking important decisions during the full moon or the no moon day.

Good Days: Monday is the most fortunate day for you, especially if you are also born on this day.

Good Dates: Dates that suit your own number are the 2nd, 11th and 29th or the dates belonging to 1, 4, 7 series.

Health: You must take care of your digestive system, throat and lungs. Avoid stress and strain as you are prone to depression. Fasting on Mondays or abstaining from speech on a full moon day will benefit you. Yoga, meditation, morning walks, massages and healing therapies will benefit you.

Relationship with Other Numbers

Fate number 1	Ideal romance partner
Fate number 2	Ideal romance partner
Fate number 3	Good as friends, but not as spouse
Fate number 4	Relationship can be difficult
Fate number 5	Relationship can be difficult
Fate number 6	Good as friends and lovers, but not as spouse
Fate number 7	Good romance partner and friend
Fate number 8	Neutral relationship, 8 benefits more than 2
Fate number 9	Ideal romance partner

Favourable Colours: All shades of green, cream and white are favourable for you.

3 This is the fate number of those born on the 3rd, 12th, 21st and 30th of any month. You are influenced by Jupiter which governs the period between 21 February

and 21 March and between 21 November and 21 December.

This is one of the most favourable fate numbers. You are ambitious and highly individualistic. Your tremendous energy and initiative drives you ahead and brings you success. You are authoritative and dislike working in any subordinate position. You are suited to working in large projects in positions where you wield executive authority. Your courageous, self-confident and dedicated nature enables you to complete any job you undertake successfully.

You receive a lot of love and guidance from friends, relatives and people in authority. You may face problems in the earlier part of your life. Though you may not believe in ceremonies or rituals, you are religious at heart.

You have a melodic voice and literary talent. You will excel in the arts and entertainment. You have moments of self-doubt, especially when you sense that you are being manipulated by others. You are an extrovert and adore attention.

You may however be an egotist. You are kind and easily moved by other people's troubles. You have a strong sense of justice and may espouse the cause of the underdog. However, you do not submit to forcible demands made on you. You are very outspoken and may have critics and enemies. Though you are quite popular with opposite sex, you are selective in your relationships. You are strongly devoted to your family. You are fond of travelling and gain a lot by it. You resent any kind of domination or hypocrisy. However, you may overemphasize creativity or be an intolerant taskmaster.

As a friend and business partner you are extremely dependable and do not make promises that you cannot fulfil. You make enemies by being dictatorial and insisting on carrying out your own ideas. You love order and discipline. You will rise to the highest position in whatever profession you are in, especially in the army, navy or government and in all professions involving trust and responsibility. You are very diligent in carrying out your duties. You are proud and dislike taking favours from others. As you are exceptionally independent-minded, you dislike any restraint. You have a very positive and optimistic approach to everything. There is a strong chance that you love sport. You are dedicated to your pets. Those born on 12th have greatest magnetism of personality.

Precautions: You must avoid arguments and unproductive discussions. Exercise control over your temper. Avoid being overly ambitious, too optimistic or dictatorial.

Strong Periods: The best period for you is between 19 February and 20 March and between 21 November to 20 December.

Weak Periods: October and November are not favourable for starting any new projects and journeys. This is a period during which Jupiter is weak.

Good Days: Thursday, Friday and Tuesday are the most favourable days for you, especially if you are also born on these days.

Good Dates: The dates that are favourable to your own number are the 3rd, 12th, 21st and 30th of any month. The series of numbers that is favourable to you is the 6, 9 series, i.e. the 6th, 9th, 15th, 18th, 24th and 27th of any month.

Health: You may suffer from sciatica and skin trouble. You must be careful of your health in the months of June and September, especially of your blood. You are susceptible to arthritis, heat eruptions, jaundice and overstrain of the nervous system.

Relationship with Other Numbers

Fate number 1	Good as friends and spouse
Fate number 2	Good as friends, but neutral in romance
Fate number 3	Good as spouse
Fate number 4	Neutral relationship
Fate number 5	Good as friends
Fate number 6	Harmonious relationship
Fate number 7	Neutral relationship
Fate number 8	Neutral relationship, not good as spouse or business partners
Fate number 9	Good as friends and spouse

Favourable Colours: Yellow, mauve and violet are best suited to you.

4 This is the fate number of those born on the 4th, 13th, 22nd or 31st of any month. You are influenced by the sun and Uranus. The influence of Uranus gives you a distinctive character, marked by originality and inventiveness.

Your behaviour is unconventional and you see things from a different point of view from everyone else. You have your own belief system and rules which do not match those laid down by society. Though you are not quarrelsome by nature, you provoke opposition and have a number of secret enemies who work against you.

Many unexpected events keep happening to you. You are seldom be understood by your friends and family. Many people consider you eccentric, and are shocked by your speech and actions.

You are intuitive and seem to always know what is

going to happen in the future. You are fixed in your habits and tastes. You become very stubborn when others try to dictate things or make you change. There are pressing domestic difficulties you have to face. But the family means a great deal to you and you never let them down. Others may try to take advantage of you, but you have to learn to handle that. Short trips and holidays are important for you.

If you are in a business partnership, it is important for you to be the leader or have a controlling stake in the actual management. You should choose your lover or spouse carefully.

You are secretive and do not make friends easily. However, your friends are always reliable. You always espouse the cause of the underdog which makes you unpopular. As you are highly strung and sensitive you get easily hurt and become isolated.

You are, as a rule, more or less indifferent to accumulating money, but you may spend lavishly and surprise people by the way you put your money to use. Reward and recognition are assured in the latter part of your life. Your finest quality is your tolerant attitude, and you expect the same from others. You are suited to occupations requiring physical endurance.

Precautions: You must learn to appreciate others. Avoid loneliness and isolation. Do not trust others blindly. You must try to decide things quickly and independently. Try to develop a more uncritical nature and do not doubt everything.

Strong Periods: The best period for you is between 21 March and 21 April and between 15 July and 15 August.

Weak Periods: The months of October, November and December are not favourable for you. You may have losses or face many obstacles in your work during this period.

Good Days: Saturday, Sunday and Monday are the most fortunate days for you, especially if you are also born on these days.

Good Dates: Dates that are favourable to your own number are 2, 4, 7 series, i.e. the 2nd, 4th, 7th, 11th, 13th, 16th, 20th, 22nd, 25th, 29th and 31st of any month.

Health: Very often you suffer from mysterious ailments which cannot be diagnosed. You must take care of your heart and blood pressure. You may suffer from colds, coughs, anemia, depression, insomnia, headaches or pains between the shoulder blades. You may also suffer from bladder or kidney trouble. Avoid red meat and eat plenty of leafy green vegetables.

Relationship with Other Numbers

Fate number 1	Good as spouse
Fate number 2	There will be attraction but avoid relationship
Fate number 3	Good as friends
Fate number 4	Women should avoid relationships
Fate number 5	Good as friends, but not as spouse or business partners
Fate number 6	Good as friends
Fate number 7	Good as friends and spouse
Fate number 8	Good as friends, there will be attraction but women should avoid relationships
Fate number 9	Good as friends, but women should avoid relationships

Favourable Colours: All shades of blue, sapphire, khaki

and grey are suited for you.

5 This is the fate number of those born on the 5th, 14th or 23rd of any month. Mercury is a ruler of this number. The peak period is from 21 May to 20-27 June, and from 21 August to 20-27 September. Mercury is at its weakest from 21 February to 21 March.

You are versatile and possess great natural charm. You love travel and entertainment. You need to travel to satisfy your restless urges and also to gain knowledge and experience. Your restlessness can be only satisfied by excitement and change. You can enchant anyone, except perhaps those whose fate number is 3 or 8. You are very highly strung, mentally alert and agile, but you lack perseverance.

You tend to overanalyse people and situations. You must trust your intuition as analysis can ruin your relationships. You are often impulsive in your actions, but these are often successful whereas careful planning may lead to problems. You have many ideas, make inventions, and are a born speculator willing to take risks. You are free of mind and heart but you cling strongly to your freedom. Though you make friends easily, you should choose them carefully as your friendships may not last long and you may be easily deceived by people.

Avoid taking major decisions which affect your personal life when you are tense. Your adaptable personality enables you to bear any calamity with fortitude. The entertainment industry attracts you, and you will be successful in this field. Anything to do with speed, movement, travel and adventure or fashion suits your nature. You like to see a constant turnover of property. You can quickly perceive the true nature of people. In business too, you can easily identify problems and make corrections. Music stirs you up and you like to be surrounded by different kinds of people. People always think that there is a certain magic about you. Though you are not averse to being in the spotlight, it is not something you strive for.

It is difficult for you to settle down to one stable relationship without having many experiences. Ideally therefore you should marry late. Certain differences with your partner are possible.

Professions suitable for you are writing, advertising, public relations and publishing.

Precautions: You must stop hurrying all the time. Try to relax and calm your mind. Stop being over-critical and avoid misjudging people. Exercises to develop self-confidence will be beneficial to you. Try to be more patient with your friends and family members.

Strong Periods: The best period for you is between 21 May and 20 June and between 20 August and 21 September.

Weak Periods: The months of May, September and December are not favourable. You may feel lack of energy, become unduly worried, lonely or withdrawn. You may also incur financial losses and debts.

Good Days: Wednesday and Friday at the most fortunate days for you, especially if you are also born on these days.

Good Dates: Dates favourable to your own number are the 5th, 14th or 23rd of any month.

Health: You are susceptible to exhausion of the nervous system, headaches, neuritis and mental restlessness. As you are prone to impurities of blood and skin problems, you must drink plenty of juices. Adequate quiet and long walks are essential to maintain good health. You may suffer from insomnia in your weak periods.

Relationship with Other Numbers

Fate number 1	Good as friends but not as spouse
Fate number 2	Neutral relationship, not good as spouse
Fate number 3	Good as spouse and friends
Fate number 4	Temporary relationships only
Fate number 5	Good as friends and spouse
Fate number 6	Good as friends, spouse and business partners
Fate number 7	Temporary relationships only
Fate number 8	Not good as friends, spouse and business partners
Fate number 9	Good as friends and business partners, as spouse only if spiritually inclined

Favourable Colours: All shades of grey, white and turquoise are suited for you.

6 This is the fate number of those born on the 6th, 15th and 24th of any month. You are influenced by Venus, which is in its peak strength when situated in the sign of Pisces (21 February to 21 March). It is at its weakest between 21 August and 22 September. If you are born in the planetary hour of Venus (see p. 195), the influence of the number will be even more powerful.

The influence of Venus makes you emotional, loving and polite. It also makes you creative and inventive, and gives you an interest in hypnotism, tantra and medicine.

You have an extremely magnetic personality. You are a very social person and cannot live alone for a long time. You are fond of adventure, and love to travel to foreign lands. Love, affection, stable personal relationships, peace and harmony are very important to you. Your abhor promiscuity. As you are determined in carrying out your plans, you appear to be very obstinate and unyielding.

However, in matters of the heart, you become deeply attached, and are a slave to those you love. You are sensual by nature.

Your emotional and highly imaginative nature prevents you from concentrating on any subject or settling in one place for long. You will always receive help from people in authority, often from unexpected sources.

There is a tendency to indulge in extravagance and to brood over personal relationships, which you must curb. You should adopt a broad-minded approach. Once roused to anger you brook no opposition. You fight strongly for causes you believe in. You are secretive by nature but can easily extract secrets from others.

Your gentle nature, refined tastes and sweet manners make you very popular. Women born under this number are very mischevious and sensual during their adolescence. You love good food, and are a good host and entertainer. Usually you will have many passing relationships before you settle down to a stable one. Many ravishing beauties, designers, artists and dancers are born under this number. Women retain their youthful vigour up a considerable age and are also very lucky for their husbands.

You will be prone to accidents but shall miraculously escape from getting killed. This is a fortunate number for gaining happiness and love from the opposite sex. You will be attracted to the occult sciences. 2 and 5 in your birth date gives you intuitive powers. You love beautiful things and are fond of rich colours, paintings, music, jewellery, designer clothes and a luxurious lifestyle. You will be attracted to artistic, learned and spiritually inclined people. Professions suitable for you are tourism, films, modelling, fashion designing, interior decoration, writing and singing.

Precautions: You must avoid arguments and the company

of negative-minded people. Resist the tendency to lose your patience and becoming agitated. You must be careful in judging people before entering any kind of physical or financial relationship. Do not rush into hasty conclusions. As you are susceptible to addiction, you must keep away from all kinds of stimulants and intoxicants. Breathing exercises, walks and massages will be beneficial for you.

Strong Periods: The best period for you is between 21 April and 21 May and between 21 September and 21 October.

Weak Periods: During May, October and November you may lack energy and interest. You may be under stress and your health may also suffer. It is advisable to be extra cautious with starting any new ventures or making investments. You may also have arguments and encounter obstacles in work.

Good Days: Friday, Tuesday and Thursday are the most fortunate days for you, especially if you are also born on these days.

Good Dates: Dates favourable to your number are the 6th, 15th, 24th, 3rd, 12th, 21st, 30th, 9th, 18th and 27th of any month.

Health: You must take care of your throat, nose and lungs. You must guard against kidney or urinary problems. There is a tendency towards exhaustion due to overindulgence. If 6 is repeated in your date of birth, it is bad for your nerves and mental well-being.

Relationship with Other Numbers

Fate number 1	Good as lovers, not as spouse or business partner
Fate number 2	Good as friends and business partners, not as spouse
Fate number 3	Good as spouse and business partners
Fate number 4	Avoid relationships
Fate number 5	Good as friends and business partners
Fate number 6	Good as spouse, friends and business partners
Fate number 7	Not good for spouse or lovers
Fate number 8	Not good for spouse or lovers
Fate number 9	Good as spouse, friends and business partners

Favourable Colours: White, pink, rose and all shades of blue are beneficial to you. You must avoid wearing black, dark purple, red and crimson.

7 This is the fate number of those born on the 7th, 16th and 25th of any month. You are influenced by Neptune and the moon. The moon is in peak strength in the sign of Taurus (21 May to 21 June) and in its own sign when transiting Cancer (21 June to 21 July). The influence is especially strong if you are born on Monday. The moon is weak when passing through Scorpio (21 October to 21 November). If you are also born in the planetary hour of the moon (see p. 195), its influence is even more powerful.

As you are born under the influence of Neptune, you extremely independent. This is a good number for those who are spiritually inclined. You are an idealist living in an imaginary world. Though you possess a strong reasoning mind and are analytical, your greatest fault is in underestimating your own individuality. Your nature will make you seek the deeper meaning of life.

Your reserve may make people misunderstand you. You plan big, but these plans are seldom translated into reality. You might face many setbacks early in life and your education may be interrupted. You are naturally inclined towards literary and research activities. In your youth you are highly impressionable, and romantic interludes will distract you from excelling in your profession.

Though you are very original in your thinking, your performance is dependent on your moods. You are of a very restless nature and unable to stay confined to any place or situation for a long time. You are very talkative and love to have discussions and debates. The influence of the moon makes you kind-hearted, sentimental and romantic.

You can be a good writer, painter or poet. You shall achieve remarkable success in creative fields. You have a leaning towards philosophy and occultism, and usually have remarkable dreams. You will have unusual experiences. You have strong intuitions and must always follow your hunches. You do not encourage favoritism, and maintain a cooperative and supportive attitude with everyone.

Large expanses of water attract you and you derive immense satisfaction from nature. You are interested in matters concerning the sea. Love of change makes you travel extensively to far-off lands, which also is gainful for you. Your magnetic and charming nature makes you popular. Success is generally achieved around the age of thirty-four. You are not very materialistic but may become rich by your own original ideas or methods of business. But owing to your philanthropic nature, you are likely to make large donations to the needy. Women are very emotional and sensitive, and even if you marry well you shall always be anxious about the future. This number is associated with inventors, musicians and composers. There is also likelihood of your friends deceiving you.

You may be restless and indecisive, but given correct

guidance, you can become extremely successful. As you are very individualistic you must not enter into any partnerships. You are better in the organizational side of business than the financial. You will be lucky in dealings in real estate. You must keep away from drugs and alcohol as you are attracted to them.

If you use your potential positively you will be drawn to research, investigation, philosophy, mysticism and meditation. However, this may make you reserved and unadaptable. If 1, 2 and 7 are repeated in your date of birth, you will achieve fame, though there may be upsets on the domestic front. Repetition of 7 thrice or more will incline you to music, fine arts, research and investigation. The combination of 1 and 7 will give you interest in engineering, medicine and software technology. Many musicians, writers and mystics have this fate number.

Precautions: You must avoid being too reserved and unadaptable. Do not make decisions in a hurry. You have to avoid being excessively emotional as this tends to upset you both mentally and physically. Try to be forceful and stable. Avoid being lazy, critical and melancholic. Serious efforts must be made to overcome vacillation. Though you are fond of water, you must avoid deep waters and dangerous water sports.

Strong Periods: The best period for you is between 21 June and 21 July.

Weak Periods: January and February are not very favourable as you may meet failures, suffer financial losses and lose good opportunities. There may also be failures in love affairs.

Good Days: Sunday and Monday are the most fortunate days, especially if you are also born on these days.

Good Dates: Dates favourable to your own number are the 7th, 16th and 25th of any month. Days in the 1, 2, 4 series, i.e. the 1st, 2nd, 4th, 10th, 11th, 13th, 19th, 20th, 22nd, 28th, 29th and 31st of any month are also favourable.

Health: You may suffer from all kinds of skin diseases, melancholy and imaginary fears. Digestive problems and infections also bother you. You may also suffer from gout and arthritis. Long walks shall benefit you. You must be especially careful of your health in your weak period.

Relationship with Other Numbers

Fate number 1	Good as spouse, friends and business partners
Fate number 2	Neutral relationship
Fate number 3	Good as spouse and friends
Fate number 4	Good as spouse and friends
Fate number 5	Temporary relationships
Fate number 6	They are beneficial for you, but not you for them
Fate number 7	Not good as spouse or business partners
Fate number 8	Avoid relationships
Fate number 9	Good as spouse and lovers

Favourable Colours: To increase your magnetic attraction you must use pastel shades, pale green, light blue, white and yellow. You must avoid black.

8 This number is governed by Saturn and is the fate number of those born on the 8th, 17th and 26th of any month. The influence of Saturn is greater if you are born between 21 December and 26 February, as this is the period of Saturn.

This number represents wisdom, learning through experience, stability, patience and responsibility. It is associated with financial security, caution, restriction, self-discipline and self-control. You are normally quiet and shy. You do not push ahead, but you achieve your ambitions. True happiness will be found only when you achieve complete freedom. You will encounter change and undertake travel.

People born under this number make excellent teachers, counsellors and politicians. You may have poor health in childhood, but you grow more robust on reaching maturity. Your sense of humour is subtle and not very obvious. There are many times when you are an instrument of fate for others. If there is 2 or 5 in your birth date, you will have psychic experiences.

You are a very private person and find it difficult to communicate openly with others. Although you appear to be cold, you are devoted to those you love and trust. Loyalty and integrity are integral to all your associations. You know what it is to be lonely and need desperately to be loved. You are capable of great sacrifices for an ideal or for those who depend upon you. You need love and admiration from your partner to achieve your high ambitions.

You seek independence. You need to strike a balance between career and home, as usually the latter takes up all your attention. This number is associated with confidence, determination and mystery. You are often misunderstood, even by your closest friends and relatives, and feel intensely lonely. You have a deep nature and great strength of individuality.

You are reserved, patient, reflective, outwardly calm and well balanced. You do not like to be helped by others primarily because you prefer to do everything yourself. Although you may meet obstacles, your persistence will always win through.

There seems to be no middle path for you. Either you will be a great success or a failure. Your life is unpredictable, and unexpected changes keep you busy.

You are very caring, and face hardships to protect the interest of your friends. You have a sensual nature. You make the best of friends and the worst of enemies. You hate hypocrisy and deceit.

It is not a good fate number from a worldly standpoint. You may be called on to face great losses and humiliations. You will always feel you are different from others.

Precautions: Avoid brooding over the past and overcome your imaginary fears. Stay away from intoxicants. Do not depend upon others for help. You should never live in a house where the number adds up to 4. You should instead choose the more fortunate vibration of a number that adds up to 6.

Strong Periods: The periods between 20 September and 21 October and between 20 January and 21 February are good for you.

Weak Periods: The months to be careful about ill health and the bad effects of overwork are January, February, July and December.

Good Days: Saturday is your lucky day. Sunday and Monday are also important days. Your energy levels are much higher on these days.

Good Dates: Dates favourable to you are the 1st, 10th, 19th and 28th of any month as well as the 6th, 15th and 24th of the month.

Health: You may suffer problems of the liver, pancreas and intestines. You may also be prone to headaches or rheumatism. You must avoid eating animal or canned food as much as possible, and live on fruits, herbs and vegetables. You may suffer from constipation and flatulence.

Relationship with Other Numbers

Fate number 1	Good as lovers
Fate number 2	Good as spouse and lovers
Fate number 3	Good as lovers
Fate number 4	Temporary relationships unless planetary influence fortunate
Fate number 5	Avoid relationships
Fate number 6	Good as lovers
Fate number 7	Good as spouse and lovers
Fate number 8	Temporary relationships unless planetary influence fortunate
Fate number 9	Temporary relationships unless planetary influence fortunate

Favourable Colours: To increase your magnetic vibrations use dark greys, dark blues, purple, indigo, navy blue and black.

9 This is the fate number of those born on the 9th, 18th and 27th of any month. This number is ruled by Mars which governs the period between 21 March and 21 April and between 21 October and 21 November.

You are a born fighter. You have difficult times in your earlier years. This number is associated with originality, aggressive action and initiative. You have great courage and determination. Once your mind is made up, nobody can stop you from getting what you want. There is a tendency to be impulsive about decisions, which you may later regret. It is common for your temper to flare up frequently, but you readily forget and forgive. You resent criticism and interference, which you often receive from others due to your dominating nature.

You may experience many disagreements in your family life. But for sympathy and affection you can do anything.

Mars makes you adventurous, but also vulnerable to fires and explosions. You may undergo surgery.

Being a natural leader, you cannot work in subordinate positions and do not like being asked to account for your conduct. You are always shocked by people who are devious and manipulative, as you are incapable of such behaviour. Mars gives you the ability to see straight to the heart of the situation, without prolonged analysis. You have a great desire to travel.

You have a charismatic personality. You are always obsessed with health and hygiene. You show a consistent ability to outshine and out-think your colleagues. You are intolerant of slow thinkers. Impatience is one trait your find difficult to control. You have an explosive temper when criticized. Truth, honesty and justice are very important to you.

You are a good parent, but family feuds may develop when the relatives interfere with the upbringing of your children. You usually get what you want by catching the opposition off guard. You have a strong tendency toward vanity. Though you seem very assertive, you are in need of continual reassurance. When you work for others, your intuition and wisdom will give wonderful results. If you work for personal profit and power you shall suffer. Any profession requiring imagination and creativity are suitable for you, such as writing, publishing, theatre, art and tourism.

Precautions: You must avoid extremes. Unnecessary conflict with your superiors should be avoided. You must overcome restlessness and lack of self-discipline.

Strong Periods: The best period for you is between 21 March and 21 April and between 21 October and 21 November.

Weak Period: During May, June, October and November, you may experience obstacles on personal, health and career matters. You must avoid any new ventures during this period.

Good Days: Tuesday and Friday are the most fortunate days of for you, especially if you are also born on these days.

Good Dates: Dates favourable to your number are the 9th, 18th and 27th of any month and also dates in the 3, 6, 9 series.

Health: You are inclined to suffer from all kinds of fevers, skin eruptions, cuts and boils, ulcers and diseases of liver and the stomach. You must strictly avoid the use of intoxicants, drugs and stimulants.

Relationship with Other Numbers

Fate number 1	Good as spouse, lovers and business partners
Fate number 2	Ideal as lovers, spouse and business partners
Fate number 3	Good as spouse and lovers
Fate number 4	Not good as spouse
Fate number 5	Neutral relationship
Fate number 6	Good as spouse and lovers
Fate number 7	Good as spouse and lovers
Fate number 8	Not good as spouse
Fate number 9	Good as spouse and lovers

Favourable Colours: Crimson, red and pink are best suited to you.

Special Advice for Fate Numbers 4 and 8

If your fate number is 4 or 8, then you will find that important events in your life take place on days in this series. If you find 4 and 8 recurring in your life, you must try to consciously avoid them.

Instead you should use the stronger numbers 1, 10, 19 and 28 as dates for important events or as the address for your house. The other dates which are also good for you are the 2nd, 7th, 11th, 16th, 20th, 25th and 29th.

By some strange law of magnetic vibration, people with the fate numbers 4 and 8 attract each other. Though you may be devoted to each other in times of trouble, this combination is not lucky in material terms.

If you decide to use your own numbers in the 4, 8 series, you may achieve success and fame, but your life may be marked by unfortunate or tragic events.

You must never try to increase the power of these numbers. Use alternative numbers such as 1, 3, 5 and 6, and think of yourself as that number and plan your life accordingly. By this you may avoid the bad luck you persistently experience.

Your Destiny Number

The date of birth (day, month and year) when reduced to a single digit is called the destiny number or the fadic number. This is the most important number in all numerological calculations. Some numerologists also call it the life path, the birth path or the talent number.

The destiny number represents your natural characteristics, both positive and negative. It also indicates opportunities, challenges and lessons which you will encounter. It represents the tools in hand, whereas the karmic compound number represents the work to be accomplished, the environment and opportunities that you will have and the final shape your life will take.

As these two numbers work together throughout one's life, success and happiness depends on their synchronization. If these numbers are in harmony, your life will be smooth and successful. If not, there will be many conflicts, delays and disappointments.

If you believe in karma, you will attribute success achieved in this life to what you have earned in your past lives. In this case, your destiny number, while it affords you little freedom of action, helps you to reap the fruits of your actions in your past lives. It is thus the record of what you have done and learnt during all your past incarnations and their vibrational patterns. This number gives insight into your life and purpose. If your destiny number is not a good one, you can use your name to counteract the negative forces.

How to Calculate Your Destiny Number

The single digit number derived by the addition of the day, month and year of birth is called the destiny number. Thus if you were born on 28 November 1968, your destiny number will be calculated thus:

11+28+1968=2007

2+0+0+7=9

Therefore, your destiny number is 9. Alternatively, you can calculate it thus:

1+1+2+8+1+9+6+8=36

3+6+=9

The advantage of the second method is that the unreduced sum can indicate your future if you refer to the chapter 'Your Karmic Compound Number'. In the above example, the destiny number is 9, but the unreduced digit is 36. The significance of 36 is given in that chapter.

What Your Destiny Number Indicates

1 This is a good destiny number promising the achievement of long-term ambitions.

You are known for your powers of leadership, strong will, independent mind and initiative. As you are ambitious and domineering, you are not suited to work in subordinate positions. Though you are popular among your colleagues, you work best when alone. You must learn to cultivate patience, as you cannot tolerate inaction or delay. You are also inclined to be self-centered and quick tempered. You should learn to cooperate with everyone without losing your individuality. You will be forced to take responsibility for your own life and actions, despite encountering manifold problems along the way.

Generally people with this destiny number are

idealistic, helpful, popular and invite attention. Government officials favour you. You may get into trouble because of your behaviour, especially displays of arrogance. Your love life may be frustrated due to your determination to lead. If you are in politics, you will occupy high posts. When you write you are original and very clear in expression. If you are in business, you will make your fortune when you are between thirty-five and forty-six years of age. Try to control your temper, especially when you have to take orders from others.

If your fate number is also 1, you will quickly achieve success in your field of week. However, to be successful, you must also have the influence of the numbers 3, 6 or 9 in your date of birth. Be careful in taking decisions in the months of October, November and December, when the sun is weak.

This is not a fortunate destiny number in matters of love and marriage. However, your friends will be devoted and dependable. You need to avoid overindulgence, avoid excessive strain and learn to relax and rest. Professions you should consider are marketing, advertising, teaching, engineering and aviation.

2 As this number is influenced by the moon you may face many ups and downs.

As you are very sensitive to your environment, you get easily discouraged by external circumstances. It is very important for you to be aware of the need to love yourself. You should choose confident and aggressive companions. You dislike being hurried into actions. You are highly imaginative and will be able to make a mark in the arts or in creative fields. Your awareness of the duality of human experience increases throughout your life. Partners and companions will influence you greatly, so choose them carefully.

There may be many changes in your personal life, if

men, elderly women or women in key positions help you. Though very loving, you are undemonstrative. When 2 is repeated in your date of birth, a great deal of changeability is indicated and you will not be able to remain in one place or profession for long.

This destiny number indicates that you have to dedicate your life to service. You will not achieve fulfilment until you develop the ability to see through the duality of happiness and unhappiness.

If you have 2 and 9 in your date of birth you have a healing touch. A love of music or musical ability is also often found. From middle age you will get deeply drawn to occult sciences, philosophy and spirituality. You will achieve the best results when working quietly. Since the moon is dominant in your life, you will benefit more from work done for others than working for yourself. Your work will bring you in direct touch with many people.

Romantic attachments will bring you joy. Children play an important role in your life. As you are of a quiet nature, you detest quarrels and prefer compromise to confrontation. Your sympathetic nature makes you an ideal homemaker. Learn the power of silence. The professions ideal for you are in government, art, literature, theatre, music, diplomacy, politics, medicine, psychology and finance.

3 This is not a good destiny number as you overload yourself and develop stress. You face many situations where urgent action is required or where you cannot exercise free well. You may often feel frustrated as rewards are long overdue and punishment comes unexpectedly.

You confuse the good with the bad because you lack discrimination. This creates disorder in your life, and your outspoken and critical nature increases the problem. You should avoid disputes as sometimes you have to incur unnecessary expenditure to placate agitated friends and family. Though blessed with creativity, intuition and eloquence you do not get due success in the early part of your life when you desire it most.

You appreciate good food and like to live well. You enjoy travel. You need to express yourself creatively. You have a decided attraction towards laughter, entertainment and the lighter side of life. Usually you are an excellent conversationalist, possess an active brain and are always full of ideas. However, you lack the motivation to put them into play. Your friendly and outgoing nature wins you many friends. Do not use these qualities negatively. Your wide range of interests may mean that you never pursue anything seriously. This lack of purpose distresses people close to you. You need to guard against overindulgence in alcohol, drugs and sex.

You must cultivate a sense of humour and mingle with people. You must also develop patience as you are apt to be impulsive and intolerant. You must not worry.

Accept things as they are and try to make others happy. Persons with this destiny number have usually a sense of dignity, can handle situations without loss of face, and often succeed by sheer charm of personality. Your intuition, which is seldom wrong, enables you to form sound judgements. Optimism shines through your life. However, do not allow this to become extreme as it may lead to of extravagance and overconfidence. You may also have a tendency to ignore the unpleasant facts of life. Avoid being hypocritical or judgemental. Professions for which you are best suited are publishing, business, publicity, the arts, interior decoration, advertising, writing, higher education, research or tourism.

4 This is a difficult destiny number. Your life is marked by sudden changes which overthrow your plans. You

must therefore keep your plans flexible as you will frequently need revise them. Your financial plans may also go awry unexpectedly and you have to think along new lines.

You may change jobs or professions frequently as you are not easily satisfied with what you are doing. You may have secret enemies because of your unconventional nature. There may be many occasions when you do not get due recognition for your efforts, and encounter opposition and criticism. Delay makes you impatient. Your strong belief in the logic of the material world may lead you to ignore the spiritual.

There are two distinct personality types among people with this destiny number. The first group is eccentric and unpredictable, but also independent, well-informed and versatile. The second group values security and stability more than originality. They do not like to take risks and prefer conventional careers and lifestyles. You may have a suspicious nature which can impair your family life. You must try to change your obstinate nature. You need to learn to relax, failing which you will suffer from nervous troubles. Learn to be patient, dependable and accurate, and you will reap the reward of success. Professions in which you will do well are as an accountant, teacher, businessman, chemist, architect, manufacturer and doctor.

5 This destiny number is associated with good luck. You are versatile, intelligent and progressive, and dislike routine. Travel and entertainment give you pleasure and profit. You are a quick thinker and take fast decisions.

Your talkativeness and unreliable attitude make people suspect your loyalty and intentions. However, your alert mind and enterprising nature brings you good openings. You take risks only when you feel secure.

Security is very important to you which is why you are likely to save rather than spend. You work well under stress.

Your greatest asset is your ability is to see people as they are, and you have no trouble accepting them that way. You like to dabble in many things. You may get money through lotteries, inheritances and business. You usually find favour from those in authority, friends and relatives. You prefer outside work to office work. You are a shrewd tactician and dislike getting involved in work which carries restrictions.

You cannot stick to one thing and are prone to frequent changes in your occupation, residence and even marital status. Travel improves and widens your commercial activities. You must form partnerships based on mental affinities. Distant contacts maintained by correspondence will result in the formation of important associations and significant gains.

Though you are quite knowledgeable you lack the patience to pursue a subject in depth. You are usually a good conversationalist and writer.

Your main problem is that you magnify trifles resulting in needless worries. You are inclined to suffer from headaches, neuralgia and insomnia. You are successful in love affairs. To achieve spiritual growth, you need to control your senses. Another negative characteristic is a tendency to overindulgence in sex, drugs and alcohol. Occupations suitable for you are writing, publicity, advertising, teaching, acting and travel.

6 The main characteristic of people with this destiny number is responsibility. Much importance is attached to family and partners. You are sympathetic, loyal and idealistic.

You will have a harmonious and fortunate background and become immensely popular with your associates. But you need to be very focussed in life as there is a tendency to abandon your own personal interests in favour of others. Partnerships are more beneficial to you than working independently. As a friend you are extremely loyal, and make friends for life. But you must guard against worry about the future.

This destiny number may create many sexual problems, especially for women. There is a tendency to enter into sexual relationships rashly. You have to get rid of this tendency by using your sense of discrimination. You may not be faithful in marriage, as you are in constant search for your soul mate. You must marry early. You have many material comforts and luxuries. You also have friends and good social contacts. You love music and dancing.

You are inclined to live a purposeful life and have all the right values. Occult sciences, tantra and witchcraft attract you. You must guard against chills and throat infections and should lead a more vigorous outdoor life. Professions which are suitable for you are interior decoration, the arts, restaurants, real estate, medicine, music and teaching.

7 This destiny number indicates that you will use your intuitive powers to good effect. You are able to easily analyse characters and situations. However, you should not exhaust your powers and must ensure periodic rest. If you do not, you will become hasty and irritable.

Between the ages of thirty and forty-five your intuitive powers increase and you may develop clairvoyance. This destiny number does not guarantee happiness as your restless nature creates misunderstandings. However, you shall command respect, not only from friends but also from enemies. Potential dangers are spending too much time daydreaming, speculating and indecisiveness. Though you are secretive, you have the ability to help or heal. You are sensitive to noise and need peaceful surroundings to perform well. Though you might have good organizational capacity, you do not have the patience to handle details, especially in financial matters. You may experience a lot of problems till the age of thirty-five, but subsequently things start improving. Although this is a materialistic number, it implies loss and sacrifice. Try to be focussed and not fritter away your energy by paying attention to too many different things simultaneously.

You are not cut out for partnerships as you are moody, but if you manage to forge an understanding, it is successful. You must try to be more extrovert. You are popular with the opposite sex. Professions for which you are especially suited are as a scientist, lawyer, teacher, writer, occultist, nurse, entertainer and researcher.

8 This is an unpredictable destiny number as Saturn is the controlling planet.

Your family may misunderstand you. You crave affection. Nothing comes easily and any success you achieve is only due to great efforts and perseverance. Your immense organizational skills and insight can take you to high positions. You have a strong need for power at all costs and this shapes your actions. You may have to face delays, obstacles, failures and humiliation.

You have to let go of attachments to receive rewards. You have to admit that you are responsible for your own disappointments and so these do not surprise you. If you are interested in spirituality, you might become a spiritual guru. Your career often takes precedence to home life.

There may be a scandal about some romantic relationship. Women with this destiny number often have difficulty in finding a partner. You have few friends, but they will be reliable. You have a tendency to be secretive and suspicious.

You will acquire knowledge and wisdom but only after suffering and failures. But professional success is guaranteed. Between the ages of thiry-five and thirty-seven, your problems will disappear and you will receive recognition. If you are in politics you will rise to the top. If you are assisted by others with favourable destiny numbers, like 2, 3 and 6, success is guaranteed. This number is also favourable if you deal with spiritual and occult sciences.

You must curb the tendency to boast and be rigid in your outlook. Try to be detached from small problems. You are a good judge of character and so you pick friends well. Though you are emotional, you do not reveal this openly. Luxury and comfort are very important to you. You will attain power, but there is the danger that you may abuse it or get isolated and too self-important. Ambition may become your undoing.

In business, gains will be slow and speculation is not advisable. You are not successful in matters of love, and you may earn a bad reputation because of scandals. Your married life may not be stable and there is a chance of divorce, which will involve emotional as well as financial trauma. However, you stand a good chance of making a mark on history. You possess more endurance and can cope with stress better than most people. You may suffer from loneliness and have to face lawsuits. Premature aging is also indicated.

If you become greedy you will start becoming unlucky. You may hurt those you love most. The influence of Saturn can cause major reversals in fortune, but you possess the ability to transcend them. You may suffer from rheumatism, cold and chills. You will be successful as a banker, engineer, broker, lawyer, surgeon, musician or in real estate and publishing.

9 This is one of the best and most powerful destiny numbers. It is associated with a scientific mind, wisdom and the highest expression of impersonal love. There is perfect awareness of the soul as this is the only number that contains all the other numbers within it. Those who believe in reincarnation say that people with this destiny number are evolved souls, and are in their final human incarnation.

You have a tolerant and unconventional mind. You can reach your goal if you increase your consciousness early in life. You will successful in the field of your choice, but you will have to make efforts and fight for success. You will rely more on your intuitive powers than on your intellectual abilities. You derive immense satisfaction from communing with yourself. You quickly adapt to the difficulties of life. You are good at sharing and inspire others greatly. Everything is possible and acceptable to you. You are charismatic and creative. Emotions govern many of your decisions. There is a great desire to love and be loved, and an appreciation of the feelings of others.

You must guard against your emotions getting the better of your reasoning. Avoid the tendency to sacrifice yourself needlessly. You may not be particularly good at financial matters as material things do not interest you as much as the spiritual.

You have a charitable disposition and you should choose a career where you can express this. You are well suited for any work that requires keen intuition or any kind of spiritual discipline. You are favoured by spiritual masters, artists, writers, influential women and those in power.

Your bold moves to solve issues arouse much opposition, but you finally win. If you develop a little restraint you will achieve great progress. Your friends are influential and sometimes violent. In partnerships, you are headstrong and quarrelsome but will not intentionally hurt others. You must realize that enduring peace of mind is a happier state than the transient joy of victory. You are extremely energetic, and fight your way to through life. But your single-mindedness often provokes opposition. You must try not to be too critical. You are susceptible to inflammatory conditions but you have great recuperative powers.

You naturally attract people from all walks of life. You are rarely prejudiced. You may be disappointed as you are a perfectionist and so lack the perspective to accept natural limitations. Learn to be detached from material possessions and relationships. Money comes to you through inheritance, from someone impressed by your work, or through lucky investments. You must try to be in harmony with your true nature. Only by facing your shortcomings and your strengths can you achieve a balance. The more you give, the greater will be your reward. You are a romantic at heart and are profoundly disappointed if your deep and true love is not returned. You will achieve great fame if you do not seek it for selfish motives. You will do well in literary and research activities.

Your Birth Chart

People having the same destiny numbers can be different due to subsidiary influences present in your date of birth which can strengthen or weaken your destiny number.

Your birth chart is a nine-square box where each number has a fixed place.

3	6	9
2	5	8
1	4	7

The top row (3, 6 and 9) represents the intellect. The middle row (2, 5 and 8) represents the emotions. The bottom row (1, 4 and 7) represents the practical sphere.

When you fill in your birth date, there will be some boxes left empty. Arrows can be drawn joining either empty boxes or the filled boxes, which reveal particular talents or shortcomings. For example, the presence of three successive numbers in one row highlights a particular strength and the absence of three successive numbers in any row reveals an area of weakness. These are called the Arrows of Pythagoras.

If your date of birth is 21 March 1969, your chart will look like this:

3	6	99
2		
11		

The figures are placed in their respective fixed positions. As 1 is repeated in the date of birth, it is written twice in the chart. Similarly, 9, which is repeated, is also entered twice.

YOUR INTENSITY NUMBER

The most frequently repeated numbers in your birth chart are your intensity numbers.

What Your Intensity Number Indicates

1 This is a number of self-expression. A single 1 in your chart indicates you are a good speaker, but find it difficult to express your real feelings. You may have difficulty in seeing the other person's point of view.

If you have two 1s in your chart, you have an objective and balanced outlook towards life and are not only able to express yourself well, but you also understand the viewpoints of others.

If you have three 1s in your chart, you are a very talkative person, though you can also be introspective and quiet depending on the situation. This combination is often noticed in the charts of optimistic, talented, outgoing people and entertainers.

If you have four 1s in your chart, you will be misunderstood frequently, though you are sensitive and caring. Clear verbal expression may also be a problem.

More than five 1s in the chart implies a lot of difficulty in verbal expression, though you may diversify into other forms of expression like painting, writing or dancing. If you do not get the opportunity to express yourself, you may seek relief in overeating, drugs or alcohol.

2 This number belongs to the emotional plane and indicates your intuition and sensitivity. If you have

only one 2 in your chart, you are sensitive and intuitive but are also liable to be easily hurt. You prefer to work in a peaceful rather than competitive environment. You can read people at a cursory glance.

If you have two 2s in your chart, you are very sharp, intuitive and sensitive. You will be able to make practical use of the good intuition and assess people well.

If you have three 2s in your birth chart, you are extremely intuitive and sensitive, but can get hurt easily and withdraw into a shell. You may also have musical ability.

If you have four 2s in your birth chart, you will be oversensitive and lonely. Due to your impatience, you might overreact to situations and people.

If you have five 2s in your chart, you will always find it difficult to trust people. Lack of confidence and self-doubt will make you suffer.

3 This number belongs to the mental plane and is related to the intellect, memory and logic. If you have one 3 in your chart, you have a fertile brain with an excellent memory. Your realistic and positive approach will help you to reach your goals.

Two 3s in your chart makes you sharp, creative and imaginative. Many good writers have this combination as they are able to express their creative ideas in words. There may be a tendency to daydream. Critical ability is also seen.

Three 3s implies excellent mental ability. But your highly imaginative nature can make you live in an imaginary world. You might have problems adjusting to people.

Four 3s in the chart makes you very imaginative and impractical and thus you may have problems in coping with day-to-day life.

4 One 4 makes you practical, with an ability to work hard in an organized manner. You may have musical ability.

Two 4s give you excellent organizational skills and creative abilities. But there is a tendency to become very materialistic and neglect the other aspects of life.

Three 4s in the birth chart makes you very disciplined, organized and hard-working. But you may frequently neglect everything other than work and the material world. You may also make wrong choices in your profession.

If you have four 4s in the chart, you live totally on the physical plane. You are deft with your hands. You have troubles understanding spiritual or intellectual matters.

5 This number is always placed in the centre of the chart, and relates to freedom and emotional stability. One 5 in your chart indicates that you are caring, understanding and tolerant. You will be able to easily motivate and inspire people.

Two 5s in the chart give you enormous drive, enthusiasm and determination. You may however make blunders due to overconfidence. You need to control your emotional outbursts, which often create difficulties in your domestic life. You may be prone to overindulge in alcohol, drugs and sex.

Three 5s indicates hastiness in thought and speech which can hurt others. Though you enjoy adventure and excitement, you must not take unnecessary risks.

Four 5s in the chart makes you prone to accidents.

6 This number is always placed in the centre of the top row and has a bearing on creativity, home and family. If you have one 6 in your chart, you are very attached your family and are happiest when with them. There is indication of rich creative and artistic potential. However,

you are insecure and always worried about having to live alone. You are the most dependable person in the family and everyone counts on you in a crisis. You get easily upset if your domestic life is disturbed.

If you have two 6s in your chart, you are usually overprotective, especially with children. As you are creative and have a strong aesthetic sense, you love to be surrounded by beautiful things. Artistic or musical ability is often present. Though you have creative talent, you lack confidence in your own abilities. Success comes only when you receive support and encouragement from your loved ones. You are inclined to always worry about your home and family. It takes you a long time to recover from small setbacks.

If you have three 6s in your chart, your enormous creative skills can provide release for your emotional tensions. There is a tendency to be too protective and possessive of your loved ones. You also need constant support and encouragement.

With four 6s in your chart, you find it very difficult to adapt your highly emotional nature to day-to-day life though you are highly creative.

7 This number is found in the centre of the bottom row of the chart. It is a number of sacrifice. If you have one 7 in your chart, you learn difficult lessons by loss of health, possessions and love. These experiences make you deeply interested in spiritual and metaphysical pursuits. A single 7, without 3 or 5, will make you seek perfection and desire to search for hidden truths.

If you have two 7s in your chart, you will be deeply drawn towards the spiritual and psychic world. Your analytical brain is well suited to solve technical problems.

The more 7s there are in your chart, the more losses and disappointments you might have to face.

8 This is a number of logic and reasoning. If you have one 8 in your chart, you are very logical, methodical and good with figures. As you have a restless and active mind you find it difficult to finish tasks you have begun.

If you have two 8s in your chart, you are very perceptive, restless and do not trust people readily. You have your own ways of arriving at opinions and it is very difficult to change your mind once a decision is made. It is a great combination for success in business.

If you have three 8s in your chart, you are highly restless, rigid and materialistic which is not conducive for lasting happiness.

9 This is a mental number. If you have one 9 in your chart, there is desire for self-improvement.

If you have two 9s in your chart, you are intelligent but have a tendency to be critical of others. More exposure to society is needed to develop a broad-minded approach.

Recurrence of 9 in the chart leads to disruption of domestic harmony, as you pick quarrels with your partners. The problem is that you are guided entirely by the head and you ignore the heart. Despite your tact and diplomacy, you may become impractical. In love, you may be passive and impersonal.

The three 9s give you a lot of mental energy and make you caring and idealistic. However, you can get miserable if there are obstacles.

If you have four 9s in your chart, you are very intelligent, but find it difficult to adjust to the mundane world. Channeling the immense energies you possess can help you.

ARROWS OF PYTHAGORAS

Some numerologists believe that Pythagoras first used this system of sixteen directional arrows to interpret charts.

Arrow of intellect: This arrow is formed when the top row is filled in by 3, 6, and 9. As all these are mental numbers, you will have an excellent intellect and memory. However there is danger of too much emphasis on the intellect at the expense of emotions. You may also look down on those with inferior minds. You will be highly successful in any area which requires constant intellectual effort. Many literary giants have this arrow of intellect.

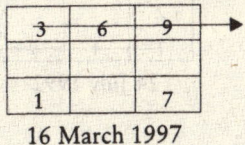

16 March 1997

Arrow of compassion: If you have 3, 5 and 7 in your chart, you have understanding and compassion. However, this is usually is accompanied by sad experiences. Strong interest in music and mysticism are often present. Acceptance of destiny allows you to be to calm and serene.

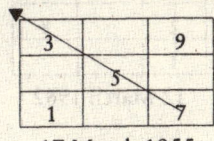

17 March 1955

Arrow of emotional balance: If you have 2, 5 and 8 in your chart, you balance the physical, emotional and spiritual aspects of life. Your understanding and compassionate nature makes you a natural healer with the ability to empathize with others. You have deep emotional needs and love is important to you.

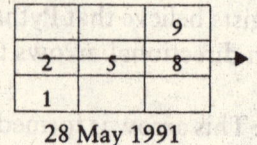

28 May 1991

Arrow of practicality: If you have 1, 4 and 7 in your chart, you are very practical and have a materialistic approach towards life. You have special skills with your hands. You shall enjoy good health and stamina.

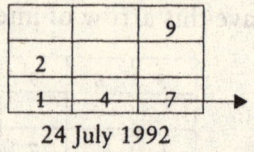

24 July 1992

Arrow of the schemer: If you have 1, 2 and 3 in your chart, you are a very good organizer as you have foresight, intuition and self-expression. Good students and communicators often have this arrow.

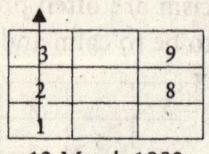

12 March 1982

Arrow of will power: If you have 4, 5 and 6 in your chart, you are extremely persistent and will be successful in reaching your goals. You are a good friend. You are able to maintain a positive attitude, despite encountering severe obstacles.

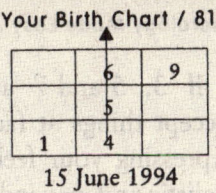

15 June 1994

Arrow of dynamic action: If you have 7, 8 and 9 in your chart, you express yourself best through action and writing. You do not postpone action once decisions are made.

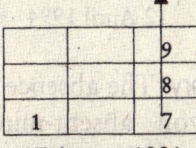

17 August 1991

Arrow of determination: If you have 1, 5 and 9 in your chart, you are very determined. Once you set your mind on something, you are patient and persistent until you achieve it. However, if 4 is missing in your birth chart, you are not able to wait for extended periods and may get disturbed.

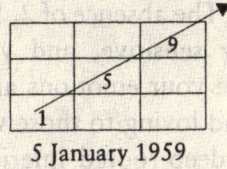

5 January 1959

Arrow of indecision: If 1, 5 and 9 are missing in your chart, you find it difficult to take decisions as you desire to please everybody. You may lack determination and motivation.

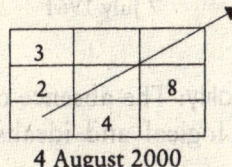

4 August 2000

Arrow of scepticism: If 3, 5 and 7 are missing in your chart, you do not accept things at face value. You might have difficulty in expressing your feelings to others. This arrow makes you idealistic and may indicate psychic ability.

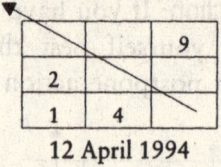

12 April 1994

Arrow of weak memory: The absence of 3, 6 and 9 in your chart will make you absent-minded and forgetful, especially as you grow older.

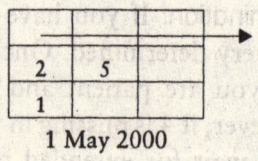

1 May 2000

Arrow of sensitivity: The absence of 2, 5 and 8 in your chart makes you highly sensitive, and you get hurt easily. However, you hide your emotions and feelings. You are very supportive and loving to those who need your help. You may have a deep-rooted inferiority complex since childhood.

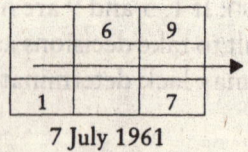

7 July 1961

Arrow of impracticality: The absence of 1, 4 and 7 in your chart makes you logical and idealistic, but thoroughly impractical.

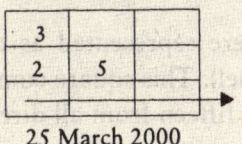

25 March 2000

Arrow of disappointment: If 4, 5 and 6 are absent in your chart, you will suffer from many disappointments and setbacks. This is due to your tendency to expect too much from others.

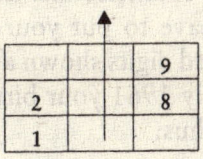

28 November 1988

Arrow of doubt: If 7, 8 and 9 are missing in your chart, you lack motivation. However, if you inculcate self-discipline your original ideas and innovative thinking will immensely benefit you.

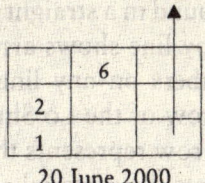

20 June 2000

THE LO SHU MAGIC SQUARE

In Feng Shui numerology the nine-star ki astrology is used with the Lo Shu magic square. According to Chinese tradition, this magic square was discovered in the markings that appeared on the shell of a tortoise when it emerged from the river Lo about four thousand years ago.

The numbers were represented as dots within the nine sections of the shell. This square considered perfect as the digits adds up to fifteen from all directions.

4	9	2
3	5	7
8	1	6

In many eastern countries this Lo Shu grid is used in numerology. You have to put your date of birth in the square as per the fixed digits shown above. For example, if you're born on 7 July 1961 your birthchart under the Lo Shu grid would be thus:

	9	
		7
	1	6

As in the previous system described, arrows are formed when numbers are found in a straight line. The presence of three numbers on any line shows arrows of strength and absence of the numbers on any line indicate arrows of weakness. The top row of the Lo Shu grid represents the intellect, the middle row represents the emotions, and the bottom row represents the material and financial plane.

Arrow of planning: This indicates a shrewd tactician or politician.

4	9	
3		
8	1	

3 April 1980

Arrow of prosperity: This indicates great material success, excellence in business and commercial ventures.

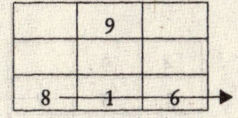

6 August 1961

Arrow of will power: This indicates a stubborn and persistent personality with strong opinions. You will successful in whatever you undertake.

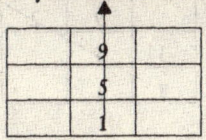

5 January 1959

Arrow of emotional balance: This indicates that you are intuitive and emotionally balanced.

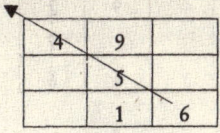

1 May 1946

Arrow of intellect: This indicates that you are an intellectual and articulate person with a good memory and a logical mind.

4 9 2
1 6

10 April 1926

Arrow of spirituality: You will have emotional harmony and spiritual values which lead to contentment after middle age.

4	9	
3	5	7
	1	

4 July 1953

Arrow of determination: This indicates that you are patient, persistent and determined.

	9	2
3	5	
8	1	

5 March 1982

Arrow of action: This means that you are always active, and fond of sports and exercise.

	9	2
		7
	1	6

2 September 1976

Arrow of weakness: This is when 2, 5 and 8 are missing. You will suffer from setbacks and failures.

4	9	
3		7
	1	6

4 March 1976

Arrow of loneliness: This is when 3, 5 and 7 are missing. This indicates lack of joy in your life. You suffer from loneliness.

	9	2
		→
8	1	6

28 October 1960

Arrow of suspicion: This is when 4, 5 and 6 are missing. You are always suspicious and negative minded.

	9	7
3		
	1	

3 July 1973

Arrow of indecision: Thi is when 1, 5 and 9 are missing. This indicates you are incapable of firmly making your mind.

4		2
		7
8		6

24 July 2006

Arrow of poor memory: This is when 2, 4 and 9 are missing. You can suffer mental imbalance, though you may be strongly intellectual in your early years.

		7
8	1	6

8 July 1886

Arrow of confusion: This is when 3, 4 and 8 are missing. You are illogical and disorganized.

	9	
	5	7
	1	6

15 June 1975

Arrow of apathy: The absence of 2, 6 and 7 indicates lack of moral and spiritual strength.

	9	
	5	
	1	

5 January 1959

Arrow of losses: When 1, 6 and 8 are missing, you will have constant failure in any scheme to make fast money.

	9	2
3	5	

23 May 2009

Your Personal Calendar

YOUR PERSONAL YEAR

At any given period of time you shall be under the influence of a number of cycles—pinnacles, name cycles, personal year, month and day cycles. The effects of the personal year cycles are more strongly felt than any other cycle.

Numerologists believe that every year has its own number and every number has its own distinct influence. In numerology, all events move in nine-year cycles or patterns. As each year contains a different energy, working in accordance with the tone of the year allows you to progress smoothly. Resisting or fighting the tone of the year will lead to disharmony and failure. Knowing the nature of your personal year will indicate the general direction to take.

The personal year cycle is of nine years and repetitive. The other cycles also change over the successive years. Some numerologists believe that some personal years—such as 1, 5, 8 and 9—have a great impact on your life and cause significant changes. Next in importance are the 4 and 6 personal years. The 2, 3 and 7 personal years are relatively less important. The personal year commences on 1 January and ends on 31 December.

How to Calculate Your Personal Year Number
To know your personal year number, add the month and day of your birth to the present year.

If you born on 6 July 1961, you will find your personal year number for year 2000 by adding the birth month to the birthday and the year 2000 and then reducing it to a single digit.

Thus 7+6+2000=2013

2+0+1+3=6

Your personal year in 2000 is 6.

Alternatively, you can simply add the birth month, the birthday and the concerned year.

Thus 7+6+2+0+0+0=15

This is reduced to a single digit. Thus 1+5=6.

To know what the year 2000 has in store for you, you should see the interpretation of personal year 6. To know your future in greater detail, you should check your pinnacles, name cycles and event number.

What Your Personal Year Number Indicates

1 This is the beginning of a new period, the commencement of a nine-year cycle. This will be a year of opportunities and beginnings. You will be more relaxed than in the previous year. This is a time to take initiatives and start new endeavours. You must be bold and take chances without becoming impulsive or headstrong. Your confidence level will be high, and your individuality and assertiveness will bring you good results. Decision-making will be much easier.

This is a year to be independent and specialize. Make efforts to promote new ideas. If you have been planning to diversify into new fields, this is the time for making that change. Whatever you do now will have a bearing on the next nine years. Do not hesitate to seek favours from those in a position to help you. On the personal front, you might lose old friends. Many separations or partings may take place. However, there will be new friends and a wider social circle.

2 As compared to the intense activity of the previous year, this year is more passive. You will need tact, patience and diplomacy. You should not be aggressive. Though you might feel that you are not getting due recognition for your efforts or that progress is slow, you must not lose heart.

This is not a good year for beginning new projects as it is a time of struggles and challenges. The vibrations are more favourable for participation in joint efforts than working alone. You should improve your knowledge through reading and research. Adopting a focussed approach will pay dividends in the future.

As you are vulnerable now, you should be discriminating and secretive. You are liable to be emotional, so do not make decisions in undue haste. Romance is in the air and new relationships will add interest to your daily routine. However, you must be selective as you may form a lifelong relationship. There may be an interesting development in connection with someone who lives overseas or by the sea. Do not allow your sentiments to cloud your judgment. Overall, this is a year of slow growth and advancement.

3 This year brings hope and growth. The thrust is on entertainment and self-expression. This is a good time to entertain friends and to enjoy yourself. As the vibrations encourage creativity, you must not lose the opportunity to develop your creative and artistic talents.

You will be very optimistic and enthusiastic, but be careful not to rush into anything as there will be delays. This is a favourable year for the growth of your finances. You should concentrate on long-term plans. Though your financial position will be very comfortable, you should keep watch on your expenditure, as there is a tendency for you to be extravagant. Sound tips from your financial consultant or stockbroker could benefit you.

Complete pending projects before taking up anything new. If you are employed, you may be transferred. Travels or a change in residence can also take place. If you are in business, you might establish new branch offices or expand. You must avail of the excellent work opportunities that come your way as you may get recognition. Overall, a year of travels, entertainment, love affairs and new friends.

4 Major changes will take place in most areas of your life. This may be the turning point in your life. This is certainly not a time to take things easy.

You will have to devote a lot of time and attention to details and routine affairs, and be organized and practical. Do not let limitations and frustration deprive you of important opportunities. Though unexpected developments will take place, they will result in your forming new associations and friendships. You must utilize the time for consolidating on past gains.

Selling and trading activities will be profitable. The period is favourable for investing in real estate or renovating your home. You should be prudent with finances. Do not neglect details. Differences with your family may result in disappointments. You need to guard your health. Conditions will start improving towards the latter part of the year.

5 This will be a most interesting year. You will be relaxed after the seriousness of the previous year. There are many surprises awaiting you. Difficulties and obstacles which you encountered in the past will suddenly vanish. This is an extremely favourable time for travel, change and variety. If you are prepared to take risks you will succeed. You must take full advantage of the new openings which lie before you.

Be interested in everything new and advertise your product as this is a time when you are required to promote yourself. You are likely to gain social recognition and must not shy away from embracing new opportunities. It is also likely that you may have to part company with those with whom you have enjoyed a close relationship in the past. A change of residence is also likely, or there may be a change in the environment or family conditions. You may travel to exotic places. This is a year to throw away conventional ways of working. You might be tempted to overindulge in alcohol, drugs and sex, therefore you must be careful.

6 Compared to the previous year this is rather uneventful with no great changes taking place. The focus is on your home and family, and you will be forced to take greater responsibility. It is also likely that there may be illnesses. You may get involved in a serious love affair which will give you immense satisfaction. This is a good year to get married. Most of your thoughts and activities will be directed towards the people you love.

Friends and partners will be amicably disposed towards you but you must not use strong-handed tactics. Important help from an influential friend will bring considerable gains. If you are in an artistic profession, you will gain recognition. Your outlook will remain easy-going and cheerful.

The vibrations of this year are favourable to buying or building a new home. Renovation or decorations at home may take place. Business will be active and profitable. The latter part of this year will bring a sense of fulfilment and satisfaction.

7 This is a rather difficult year. There will be a turning point in your fortunes due to which you may face

hardships. This is not a time for business expansion. If you do not take risks with money, this may be a reasonably good financial year. Impulsive actions will bring losses.

There is great possibility that old problems may recur. Meeting old acquaintances is also indicated. You will avoid socializing as you will be in an introspective mood. This is a good year to analyse, study and perfect whatever you are deeply interested in. Unusual events will inspire you to be introspective. You will sense the need for inner development and spend time alone meditating.

You will also become acutely aware of the need to specialize in your line of work. Your efforts towards specialization will bring you recognition. You must avoid depression though you may feel lonely. This is a year in which you have to strengthen the foundation of your life.

8 This is a year to reap the fruits of the past year. Businessmen will find big opportunities coming their way. You may buy property. There will be closure in many matters. Though the prospects for the future are good, this is not the year in which you should expand your undertakings. You will develop new relationships with those in power.

The vibration is one of expansion, growth and money. It is a time to encash on seeds sown earlier. Many matters will go your way; if you sell something it will fetch a good price, if you buy you will get a good deal. Your vision and intuition will help you in being more efficient and focussed. Overall, this will be a satisfying year.

9 This is the culmination of the nine-year cycle and a period of inner stocktaking. You should look back over the past years and let go of things that have outgrown their usefulness. You might find this difficult and painful, but you will have to take firm decisions. If you try to cling on to something which you have outgrown, it will bring disappointments.

You have to learn to be tolerant and compassionate. You may encounter losses both in friendship and business unless you try to live unselfishly. Your attitude this year will be impulsive and ambitious. You will become more direct and emphatic in speech. It is necessary to guard against extremes. You must avoid becoming involved in quarrels. You may also have a love affair and other dramatic experiences.

YOUR PERSONAL MONTH

Just you move through nine-year personal year cycles, similarly you pass through nine-month and nine-day cycles, though their impact is less than that of the personal year cycle.

How to Calculate Your Personal Month Number

You have to add the current calendar month to your personal year number.

Your personal year number is 6 and you want to find the personal month number for November. Add the two numbers and reduce the sum to one digit.

Thus 6+11+=17

1+7=8

Your personal month number is 8.

What Your Personal Month Number Indicates

1 This is a time for new beginnings. Marriage, transfers and travelling are indicated. You are bound to be action-oriented. However, this will also be a period of

hardship. You will have new ideas, and the energy and will power to execute them. There will be new opportunities. This is a good time to create new avenues of income, and to make necessary changes. You must avoid being impulsive, dogmatic, aggressive and argumentative. Wear orange, copper, red and lilac for enhancing your magnetic vibrations during the month.

2 You will have a sensitive and cooperative approach. This is a time to clear up misunderstandings with friends. Changes that take place in this month are connected to those close to you, especially your family. There may be quarrels on emotional issues or on account of ill health. You should concentrate on research, business or assignments that have occupied your mind in the recent past. You must be tactful and avoid the use of force to settle issues. Try to rest as much as possible to recharge your batteries. Avoid being moody or indifferent. This is a much more calm period than the previous month. Use the colours gold, white, yellow and salmon to increase your magnetic vibrations.

3 This is an enjoyable month unless you are in personal year 7. You will develop new social contacts, socialize, entertain friends and go for outings. You will meet old friends and acquaintances with whom you have been out of touch for a long time. This is also a time when you need to express your talent. Imaginative and creative pursuits will prosper. For those who are artistically inclined, this is a good period to hold exhibitions, fashion shows or performances. You must however avoid the tendency overspend, scatter your energy and overindulge the senses. To increase your magnetic vibrations, wear amber, wine red, forest green and rose.

4 Your energy levels will be low, so you must try to bring order in your work. There will be a change in fortunes in this month. You might feel pressured as you will find it very difficult to carry out your plans. A more practical and disciplined approach is needed. However, this is a stable period in which there are opportunities to build stronger foundations for what has already been established. To increase your magnetic vibrations, wear green, blue, brown, grey and turquoise.

5 This is a month in which you will be required to adjust your plans as changes arise unexpectedly. You will find new people and interests coming into your life. Any misunderstandings taking place in this month will be resolved soon. Be careful of what you say as ambiguous words can mar your relationships. Your emotions will fluctuate. There will be many sexual attractions. However, you may have a difficult time in love. Anything you start during this period is not destined to last long. Secrets will come out in the open, and things either be resolved or fall apart. Quarrels might worsen and there might be court cases. There may be a loss of contact with an acquaintance, either due to death or departure to a distant place. You will be resourceful, adaptable and sociable. You must guard against being temperamental and unfocussed. To increase your magnetic vibrations, wear turquoise, pink, blue or red.

6 This is one of the best times for love and marriage. The focus is on domestic matters, and circumstances will force you to accept responsibility and devote more time and energy to the family. You have to ensure that perfect harmony at home is maintained. Do not hold on to your views, try to compromise. You might be kept busy being an intermediary. This is a good time for socializing and keeping in touch with old acquaintances. You must guard

against selfishness, instability and unwillingness to adjust. Creative endeavours such as music, art and the theatre are favoured.

7 Do not start anything new, instead attend to the business at hand. Towards the beginning of the month you might feel that things have hit rock bottom and there are no solutions in sight, but something good will take place unexpectedly towards the middle of the month. Adopting a receptive approach will help you accomplish more than an aggressive and self-assertive one. You will need to spend time alone to think things out and will gain important insights. This is a good time financially and you might unexpectedly gain money which will ease your difficulties. This is also a good time for a vacation and to plan future activities. Your intuition will help you. You must maintain patience. Try to examine the practicality of all your endeavours. You will be contemplative, suspicious and possessive. To increase your magnetic vibrations, wear purple, turquoise, magenta and violet.

8 The thrust in this month will be on business. You will need to exercise greater discretion. You should turn your mind to practical and economic issues and consolidate financial security. Speculations or investments can bring good returns. The time is also good for buying and selling property. Completion of old issues will keep you occupied. Avoid being lazy and pleasure-seeking as you might miss excellent opportunities. Overall, there is an excellent business and material vibration. However, maintaining a balance between the material and the spiritual will bring success. To increase your magnetic vibrations, wear gold, blue-grey, beige, tan and green.

9 This is difficult month in which great changes take place, and you have to take major decisions and start

thinking anew of your future. There will be a realignment in your destiny patterns. There might be loss of personal belongings. You must avoid friction as rifts begun during this period become permanent. However, this is a good time to eliminate undesirable people or conditions from your life. Do not hold on to things or people who are desirous of drifting away from you. You will be required to cultivate a broader outlook. An impersonal attitude is recommended in your relationships. Avoid being hasty and getting carried away by your feelings. Your present friendships will become stronger and you shall make new friends. In all situations show compassion, broad-mindedness and understanding. This is also a month of seeking pardon and forgiving, going on a pilgrimage, and doing charity. Overall, this is an emotional and dramatic period of fulfilment. You must guard against being indifferent, aloof and insensitive. To increase your magnetic vibrations, wear red, gold, green, white, lavender and olive.

YOUR PERSONAL DAY

Each day of the year has a different vibration. Some are more favourable for sudy or research, others for seeking favours or relaxing.

How to Calculate Your Personal Day Number

Add the single-digit value of the day you want to know about to your personal month number and reduce it to a single digit.

If your personal month number is 8, and you want to find your fortunes for the 13th of that month, add the two and reduce the sum to a single digit.

Thus 8+13 = 21.

2+1 = 3.

What Your Personal Day Number Indicates

1 Begin something new. Ask for favours, and be assertive and goal oriented. Make quick decisions based on your intuition.

2 Be tactful and diplomatic. Collect your outstanding dues. Operate on a low key. Keep away from misunderstandings and consult others.

3 Entertain friends, relatives and business associates. Go shopping, express yourself creatively in writing, painting, music or acting. Play golf or bridge, or go to see a play.

4 Work hard and complete pending jobs. Be economical. Do not start anything new and desist from asking favours from the opposite sex.

5 Organize yourself. This is a good day to deal with the opposite sex and to travel. Promote new ideas, advertise your product, or try something new and unusual.

6 Make adjustments, beautify your surroundings, and be conciliatory in your approach. Organize community and educational projects. This is a day to take on responsibilities. Avoid the tendency to argue.

7 This is a day of seclusion and rest. It is favourable for spiritual rather than material success. Do not rush into things, and be at peace with yourself and others. You will get your dues if you sit still, rather than if you run around.

8 This is a day to sign big contracts, deal with large financial institutions and corporations, and apply for loans. Use tact and diplomacy in carrying out your plans. Grasp new opportunities.

9 Finish pending work and patch up quarrels. Make attempts to express your talents before the public, reach out for the masses rather than individuals. For artists this is a good day for public performances. There may be a vacation or travel.

Your Pinnacle Number

Pinnacle are the signposts on the path of your life and signify the height of achievement possible for you. They are not related to longevity, but indicate the trends and influences, experiences and changes that you will encounter at various ages.

The indications of the pinnacles are more or less unalterable. It is therefore desirable that you prepare yourself and be ready for what they indicate.

The first pinnacle governs your life from your birth to the time you reach maturity, which is between twenty-seven and thirty-five depending upon your destiny number.

The remaining three pinnacles begin at nine-year intervals. The second and third pinnacles govern your middle age. They are more productive than the first. The third pinnacle is called the age of progress. Most people finally find out what to do with their lives by the end of the second pinnacle, and actually do it during the third pinnacle. The fourth pinnacle is towards the retirement years of your life. Your life during this pinnacle depends largely on the kind of preparation you have made in the second and third pinnacles. Some numerologists state that the fourth pinnacle lasts till the end of your life.

If your soul urge number is the same as any of your pinnacle numbers, then opportunities or events will present themselves to realize your desires. If your expression number (sum of your full name) and your pinnacle number is same, then you will receive much help and success in developing your talents and abilities.

How to Calculate When Your Pinnacles Change

The first stage is to reduce the digits of your birthday, birth month and birth year to a single digit. (This is also how you calculate your destiny number.) If this adds up to 11 or 22, you should not reduce them to a single digit as these are master numbers. You should then read the influences of both the reduced and unreduced numbers.

To Calculate When the First Pinnacle Ends: Subtract your destiny number from 36. Thus, if your destiny number is 3, your first pinnacle will last upto thirty-three (36-3).

The other pinnacles come at intervals of nine years.

Destiny number	First pinnacle ends	Second pinnacle ends	Third pinnacle ends	Fourth pinnacle ends
1	35	44	53	62
2	34	43	52	61
3	33	42	51	60
4	32	41	50	59
5	31	40	49	58
6	30	39	48	57
7	29	38	47	56
8	28	37	46	55
9	27	36	45	54

How to Calculate Your Pinnacle Numbers

To Find the First Pinnacle: Add the single-digit value of your birth month to the single-digit value of your birthday, and reduce the sum to one digit.

For example, if your birth date is 15 July 1961, then

your first pinnacle will be 7 (July) +6 (that is 1+5)=13. Reduced to one digit, it will be 1+3=4.

To Find the Second Pinnacle: Add the single-digit value of your birthday to the single-digit value of your birth year.

Thus, to use the previous example, the second pinnacle will be 6 (that is 1+5)+8 (that is 1+9+6+1=17, reduced to one digit). Thus 6+8=14, which reduced to one digit will be 5.

To Find the Third Pinnacle: Add the single-digit value of your first pinnacle to the single-digit value of your second pinnacle.

Thus, to use the previous date, the third pinnacle will be 4+5. Therefore 9 will be the third pinnacle number.

To Find the Fourth Pinnacle: Add the single-digit value of your birth month to the single-digit value of your birth year.

Thus, to use the previous example, the fourth pinnacle will be 7 (July) +8 (1+9+6+1, reduced to one digit) =15. Reduced to one digit, this will be 6.

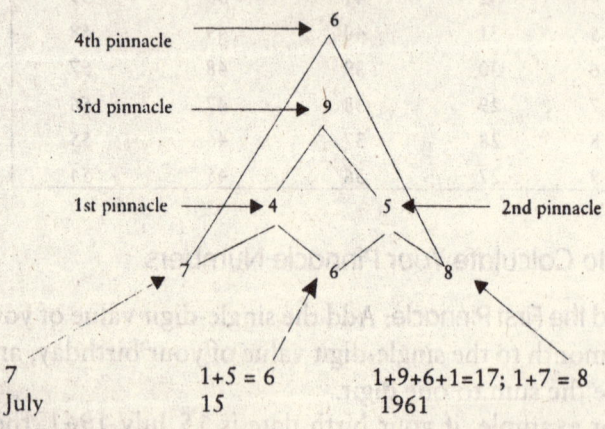

4th pinnacle → 6

3rd pinnacle → 9

1st pinnacle → 4   5 ← 2nd pinnacle

7   6   8

7   1+5 = 6   1+9+6+1=17; 1+7 = 8
July   15   1961

What Your Pinnacle Number Indicates

1 The commencement of this period will bring in many difficulties, great activity and change. You may not receive support from your family and friends. You need to keep focussed on your goals. There will be plenty of opportunities for self-improvement and growth. Circumstances will force you to exercise your will power and determination.

You must avoid being headstrong, self-centered or egotistical. You will be able to develop your individuality. You shall reap benefits if you seize the initiative. This period gives you an opportunity to be independent and on top of things.

2 This is a period where you will have to work cautiously. Any tendency to force issues will be counter-productive. You need to be diplomatic and cooperative. You might become extremely sensitive, which you will have to overcome.

Initially you may lack self-confidence. If this pinnacle occurs early, you will be oversensitive and have difficulty in expressing himself. You may have to live away from your parents. But increased awareness will make you aware of your deficiencies and you will develop a practical attitude. If you are able to keep your oversensitive nature under control, you will be successful in most projects.

Your artistic qualities will find expression during this period. If 2 is your second or third pinnacle, you will develop new associations and partnerships. Yoga and meditation will benefit you. You must bear in mind that this is a period of cooperation and diplomacy. You will have to often give way to the will of others. You will be able to accomplish a lot by working with others rather than alone.

3 This is one of the easy pinnacles. Children must make the most of it in their academic life. Self-discipline and proper channelization of talents are needed. The circumstances will be highly conducive to develop artistic, literary or theatrical talents and gain recognition.

Those passing through their second and third pinnacles will have a cheerful social life with much travel and pleasure. Your circle of friends will increase. Gain through friends is also indicated. You will be able to overcome problems effortlessly. Though you may have enjoyable love affairs, you may face heartbreak, especially if you are a woman. You must avoid the tendency to scatter your energy and money by becoming careless and extravagant.

4 This is a difficult pinnacle, requiring hard work. Circumstances will not be favourable to you. Children will be affected by the difficult financial conditions of their parents.

This pinnacle emphasizes the need to inculcate system and order in your life. Though there will be hardships and frustrations, this is also a time to lay a good foundation for the future. Sincerity and dedication will bring good results. Patience, concentration and application will be necessary to pass through the trials and ordeals of this pinnacle. Your organizing skills will be greatly enhanced. You will have to learn to be more flexible and adaptable. This is a good time to save and accumulate.

5 This is a period of changes and exciting possibilities. Children will be restless and find it difficult to apply themselves. This is a number of movement, progress and advancement.

You will realize that accepting limitations is necessary for your freedom. You must cultivate your talents, especially your speech and writing abilities.

You must not get into superficial relationships which may cause you to fear important ones. New experiences, meeting new people and travelling great distances are also indicated. This is a period of expansion of your mental horizons. If you are ready to change your approach and adjust to changes. you will be able to make substantial progress. Be careful in your dealings as there may be legal complications. You have to learn to be progressive and to discard the old.

6 The onset of this pinnacle is likely to bring in situations which demand duty and responsibility from you. There will be involvement with friends and family who will require a lot of your attention.

This is a period centred on marriage and the building of a home. You will experience love and close relationships. It is also a good time for business and financial interests. You must however guard your health. Overall, this pinnacle promises progress and growth.

7 This is a rather difficult period unless 7 is also your soul urge or destiny number. Children may suffer from isolation and repression. Financial hardship can cause problems, as can health worries. This is a period of introspection, and spiritual and mental development.

You will develop an analytical and scientific mind, which enables you to specialize in some line of work in which you will achieve recognition. You will not be inclined towards marriage and materialistic things. If 7 is your second or third pinnacle, you will develop excellent contacts with those in power. However, you may encounter problems in partnerships. In your desire to attain perfection you may become critical and isolated. Your ability to concentrate will be greatly increased. You will rely on your intuition.

Spiritual growth and increased knowledge will bring

contentment if you are older. You may suffer personal losses during this period.

8 This is one of the best pinnacles for success in business. At the onset, there may be many limitations and problems. You will have excellent opportunities to attain fame by exercising good judgment. This is a period of material growth and affluence. Your ability to organize large enterprises will give you a feeling of stability.

However you must not ignore your spiritual and human values. If your pinnacle number is the same as your birthday or destiny number you will attain recognition, get a significant promotion or quantum material gains. There will be many opportunities to accumulate money, through work and using experience gained in the past.

9 This is a karmic pinnacle. 9 is a number of selflessness. This is a period of opportunities but there will also disappointments in personal matters. You may experience several affairs coloured with emotions and drama. You need to learn selflessness and sympathy. Personal interests will bring grief.

Those involved in social activism or artistic and dramatic pursuits will gain immensely. Though this will be a good time for growth and progress in business, finances will fluctuate. You will feel an increased sense of social responsibility and be involved in charitable or philantrophic activities. You will also be attracted to religion and philosophy. Extensive travel and meeting new people from different walks of life is indicated.

11 This is powerful pinnacle as 11 is a master number. Children may be emotionally confused. This period promises enormous spiritual and personal growth. Initially, you may find it difficult to find a direction in your life. There will also be problems in partnerships and marriage. You will be highly creative and innovative. You must learn to trust your intuition. According to some numerologists, this is a time of illumination, fame and inspiration for you or your child. If this pinnacle number is the same as your date of birth you will have great spiritual awareness.

22 This is a very challenging pinnacle. For those whose date of birth is also 22, this will be a time of worldly affairs and international expansion. It is the highest possible business pinnacle.

You will face enormous challenges, both materially and spiritually. This is said to be a pinnacle of extremes. Your confidence, faith and great efforts will help you in overcoming the numerous obstacles in your path. Without hard work and sincere commitment, your ambitions will not succeed. Those of you who are passing through your fourth or last pinnacle may be involved with big projects which will keep you very busy in your old age.

Your Name and Your Fortunes

Your Name

Your name is made up of a series of numerical vibrations that contain the essence of your identity. If your name is in harmony with another person's, that person will instantly like you.

Each part of your name indicates different things about you. Your first name indicates your personality. Your middle name shows how you cope in emergencies. Your last name demonstrates your hereditary traits.

Each letter in your name has a separate vibration and influences your characteristics. Their influence depends on their position within your name. The first letter of your first name is the most important. It indicates the way that you approach opportunities and tackle obstacles. Its influence is felt more on the physical plane rather than the spiritual. The last letter of your first name indicates your ability to finish projects.

Ideally, the difference in values of the consonants and the vowels in your name should be minimum. The closer the two values are the more you are what you appear to be. The vowels reflect your mental state and the consonants your personality. If the value of the vowels is lower than that of the consonants, your personality is commanding but your inner self may not be as forceful. But if you want a well-balanced personality, there must be reasonable balance between values of the vowels and consonants.

Points to Remember About Name Analysis

- The version of your name that you use most commonly is the one you should use, rather than your given name.
- There are two tables of values used for name analysis. These are the Pythagorean table and the Kabala value table.
- For comprehensively analysing your name by numerical values, you should study the value of the vowels separately, the consonants separately and then the combined value of the two together.

The Pythagorean Table

This is used to calculate the soul urge number, the expression number, the intensity number and the event number. Most contemporary numerologists follow this set of values. This is also called the western school because most western numerologists use only this value table. It is believed that these are the original values used by Pythagoras.

1	2	3	4	5	6	7	8	9
A	B	C	D	E	F	G	H	I
J	K	L	M	N	O	P	Q	R
S	T	U	V	W	X	Y	Z	

The Kabala Value Table

There are many versions of the Kabala value table. Two have been used in this book. Traditionally, Kabala means received from God.

Kabala Value Table According to Chiero: This is based on a system fixed by the Chaldeans and passed on to the Hebrews. This system, now known as Hebrew numerology, is the oldest known to man. Tarot cards are related to this. These values have been used extensively by Cheiro and other numerologists. No letter has the numerical value 9 as this number represented the nine-letter name of God. In this book, this table is used to calculate the karmic compound number. A few numerologists have applied this to abstract entities like cities and corporations.

1	2	3	4	5	6	7	8
A	B	C	D	E	U	O	F
I	K	G	M	H	V	Z	P
J	R	L	T	N	W		
Q		S		X			
Y							

Kabala Value Table According to Sepharial: The following Kabala table has been used by the renowned numerologist Sepharial, who has done extensive research on phonetics. He claims that these values give good results, especially in determining health traits from the name. In this book, this table is used to calculate health indications.

1	2	3	4	5	6	7	8	9	10	11
A	B	G	D	E	V, U, W	Z	H	Th	I, J, Y	C, K

12	13	14	15	16	17	18	19	20	21	22
L	M	N	X	O	F, P	Ts, Tz	Q	R	S	T

What the First Letter in Your Name Indicates

A You are very independent, ambitious and original. Strong will power and leadership qualities make you assertive, enabling you to push your views through. You do not try to delude others about what your real intentions are. Try to be more diplomatic as you are too direct. You should also try to be more flexible. You dislike interference and have a tendency to act aggressively in emotional matters.

Positive A makes you creative, original, authoritative and ambitious. At the same time it can make you intolerant and self-opinionated.

Receptive A makes you idealistic and receptive to ideas but easily frustrated when unable to carry them out.

Dual A means that you have the ability to listen both sides of an idea, but you can also become a gossip-monger. You may also be indicisive.

A and E together gives you ambition, talent, understanding and power.

A and I together gives you ambition, inspiration, and illumination.

A and U together gives you great creative and intuitive powers.

A and O together makes you direct and an inspirational leader.

B You are a sensitive and emotional person. You require peace and harmony and prefer quiet surroundings. Though you are friendly, you are shy and it takes you time to open up with strangers. You are a good observer. You can be very secretive and have a tendency to be moody.

C You are imaginative, active and energetic. The repetition of C in your name will help you to tide over difficulties. You are a generous person with an optimistic attitude. Fear and anxiety make you lose your focus. You perform well in public situations.

D You are practical, methodical and patient. The danger is that you might get too involved in routine. You may become stubborn and uncompromising. Much importance is given to material things. You have few friends whom you can confide in, because of your secretive nature. More than two Ds in the name indicates limitations, which can be overcome by tolerance and patience.

EYou have a well-balanced disposition, which allows you to develop on all planes. You may also be restless, with a love of travel. You are adaptable and versatile with a great ability to communicate. You need lots of freedom. Your emotional reactions are quick.

Positive E makes you versatile, energetic and resourceful with progressive ideas. New and unusual ideas constantly attract you.

Receptive E means you are studious but restless. Your determination drives you to achieve your goals. However, you lose patience if there are obstacles.

Dual E makes you very sensitive.

E and A together gives you ambition, energy, power and success.

Two Es together means you are talented, enthusiastic, understanding and have great physical desires.

E and I together means both your mental and emotional energies combine in your actions. You are warm, receptive and shall have many relationships.

E and O together makes you inclined to spiritualism.

E and W together gives you energy, power and research abilities.

FYou are not as secure as you appear to be. You need affection, and you never forgive selfish and disloyal people. You love children and domestic life. You are responsible but need creative fulfilment in life. You have a special ability to bring harmony and ease even in difficult circumstances. Avoid interfering in the lives of others though your compassionate nature may prompt you to do so.

GYou are analytical, introspective and intuitive. Great ideas come to you on the spur of the moment. However, you need to sort out your values. You have creative potential and work hard to achieve what you believe in. Your disciplined and methodical approach and your vision may bring you success. You have self-control and great will power. You need to check your impulsive nature. You have the ability to communicate but you may choose to withdraw into yourself. Always follow your hunches.

HYou are firm, well balanced and level-headed. However, you may also be indecisive and self-centred. You may become lonely due to your own scepticism and self-doubt. You have good financial acumen and desire social recognition. This letter is powerful in the material sphere.

IYou have unusually intense beliefs and feelings. You are self-reliant and independent but very impatient when prevented from carrying out your plans. Your methods are direct, forceful, and successful. You have the ability to carry on despite opposition. You are emotional, so try to maintain a balance as otherwise you may suffer from nervous tension. You are idealistic with a romantic attitude to life. Avoid being impressionable and overdramatic. You have humanitarian instincts.

Positive I makes you direct and intense emotionally but there is danger of your becoming cruel and self-indulgent.

Receptive I makes you quiet, helpful and logical in even emotional matters.

Dual I makes you very sensitive. You need to develop your powers of communication.

I and A together indicates you have direction and illumination.

I and E together leads to fast changes by inspiration.

Two Is together indicates you are self-centred and intuitive.

I and O together indicates you are brave, sensitive, compassionate and artistic.

I and U together means you need to learn to express love clearly.

I and W together indicates there will be struggles before you reach your goal.

J You are quick to seize new ideas, and original. You are creative, perhaps talented in writing or painting. You have leadership qualities but you cannot always complete projects you have undertaken. Indecision could weaken your ability to lead. You are objective and have the knack of seeing both sides of a situation. Your attention may be diverted easily, as you are interested in too many things simultaneously.

K You are moody and want to live in an imaginary world. You have the ability to inspire others. You are emotional and creative but inhibited by nervous tension and fear. You want to be the best and your magnetic personality, coupled with your endurance and cooperative nature, help you succeed. You will be attracted to all kinds of entertainment. Always act according to your intuition.

L You have well-developed and logical reasoning powers. You prefer the lighter side of life. You are honest, sincere and straightforward. You have a good-natured disposition, and tend to give in easily. Common sense philosophy benefits you a lot. You are versatile, popular and successful. People are drawn towards you. During emotional stress you will be prone to accidents, so try remain calm.

M You are a practical and strong-willed person. You have good powers of concentration. You are well organized but you lack broad vision and are moody. You crave love and affection. Your tolerant nature allows you to endure hardships. You have a strong physical constitution.

N You are an emotional person but flexible in thought. There is great depth of feeling. You are intuitive, creative and unconventional. You have a tendency to repeat mistakes. You can achieve whatever you desire once you discipline yourself. You may receive public recognition and fame. You have a sensual nature and may have many love affairs.

O You have an attractive personality but are conservative. You are a private person and suffer from bouts of depression. You have strong will power, religious convictions and high moral standards. You love beauty and have a well-developed aesthetic sense. You easily adapt to domestic changes and will have financial stability.

Positive O indicates that you are gifted artistically and musically. Avoid becoming arbitrary and arrogant.

Receptive O is a happy letter. You will socialize a lot.

Dual O gives you tolerance and an understanding of human nature.

P You like to be aloof. Others find it very difficult to know your feelings. You have clarity of vision and foresight. You have intellectual depth and think deeply on various aspects of life. There may be many surprises in your life. You have deep interest in religion and the occult. You cannot tolerate interference. You have common sense and are practical, but you often become impatient. If there are many Ps in your name, power and success will be yours.

Q You live in two worlds, the physical and intuitive. Strong will power and determination help you to achieve your objectives. You have a practical approach and clarity of purpose. Though you have good executive ability, these will be of more use to others than yourself. You can hold positions of responsibility and inspire confidence in others. You will achieve success in business. You have good financial acumen but you can be erratic and unstable. Your eccentricity and mysterious nature make it difficult for people to understand you. Your mind is always open to new ideas and projects.

R You are very confident, and both materialistic and idealistic. You desire to make your influence felt everywhere. You are interested in the welfare of your friends, family and the community, and ready to sacrifice time and energy for them. Though you are kind, generous and helpful, you need to control your temper and be less critical.

S There are many successes and failures for those who have this letter. You instinctively search for a balanced life which is rarely achieved. Intense happiness and sudden gloom are very common with you. You are frequently confused, especially where emotions are involved. Though you know that adjustments have to be made, you have difficulty in determining what exactly these are. Your charming, charismatic and warm nature make you very popular. Try to take decisions after giving adequate thought. You are impulsive and sometimes react in an abrupt and extreme manner. You idolize only a certain kind of people, but if this devotion is betrayed you are greatly hurt. You are passionate and loving. You need success and social esteem. You are not always secure and there is a tendency to become too self-absorbed.

T You will often have to sacrifice your interests. You are very sensitive and get easily hurt, and this interferes with your judgement. You may have spiritual leanings. You are not be comfortable in competitive situations. Your anxiety to satisfy yourself and others may cause you to suffer. You tend to step back when there is a conflict of interest. You have a lot of love, tact and desire to show friendship. You thrive on affection.

UYou are expressive, with a lively imagination and are always looking for something new. You can easily be thrown off balance. Though you have an open mind and seek the truth, you cannot take decisions easily. You anticipate problems that may never materialize. You are lucky and usually happen to be at the right place at the right time. But you must be careful that you do not lose your luck through carelessness. You have imagination, charm and inspiration.

Positive U gives you writing ability and intuition. You love beauty and enjoy being with people.

Receptive U makes you selfless and shy. You will be conservative and secretive. You have the power to help others through intuitive gifts.

Dual U makes you seem indifferent because of your aloof nature.

VYou have the ability to learn anything you want to and to use power with discretion. You have to work hard, but the rewards will be gratifying. You may suffer from nervous tension. Though you are sincere, loyal and dependable, you are unpredictable in your relationships with the opposite sex. You will be materially successful. You can cut through to the heart of any matter with your intuition and insight.

WYou are very ambitious but you may have a life of ups and downs. You have a very eager spirit and take great risks. You want to live life to the full. Speed, travel, adventure and excitement attract you immensely. You are very expressive and creative, and your personality impresses everyone. But try not to postpone commitments. You have unusual power and gain victory despite great handicaps and opposition. Pleasure and change are important to you.

X You have an attractive personality. You are perceptive and have artistic talents. You may achieve public recognition. You suffer from frequent mood imbalances and depression. You are very sexual and have to guard against excesses. There is also a tendency to exaggerate your suffering in times of adversity.

Y You have a refined and stylish personality. You dislike crowds intensely. You have few friends and generally keep your secrets to yourselves. You hate limitations and restrictions. Good intuition and fine perception help you a lot. You desire the esoteric or mysterious things in life. Intellectual work suits you, but you prefer to work alone.

Z You are a very optimistic and dynamic person. Your compassionate and understanding nature make you very popular. Though you have high expectations, you are practical and down to earth. You form fixed habits. Even in the midst of severe disillusionment you maintain steady effort. You may achieve recognition. You love power and luxury. Metaphysical and occults sciences also attract you. A comfortable domestic life is important to you.

Your Karmic Compound Number

The karmic compound number shows the hidden influences in your life. It foreshadows your future and the hidden current of destiny. If you believe in reincarnation, then the significance of this number is even greater as it is believed that unlike your fate number and destiny number, the influence of the karmic compound number continues even after you leave your present body.

Harmony between your fate number and karmic compound number creates a good environment for friendships and relationships. Women often take on their husbands' surnames after marriage. The entry of an enemy number may create problems in their relationships. On the other hand, a name with a fortunate numerological value can bring good luck and happiness. The karmic compound number is the sum of the letters of your full name.

The world-famous numerologist Cheiro calculated the karmic compound number based on the sum of the full name after reducing the value of each name to a single digit. However, the unreduced name value gives a lot of information as well.

How to Calculate Your Karmic Compound Number

You need to replace the letters in your name by their numerical values according to the table of Kabala values as given by Chiero (see p.115).

Thus, if your name is Ajoy Kumar, the value of your name will be as follows:

A	J	O	Y		K	U	M	A	R
1	1	7	1		2	6	4	1	2

Sum of vowels: 15
Sum of consonants: 10
Unreduced karmic compound number: 25

Karmic compound numbers range from 10 to 73. Thus do not reduce the value of your karmic compound number to a single digit if the sum of the digits comes to less than ten.

What Your Karmic Compound Number Signifies

10 This promises honour, faith and success. In the Kabala, it is represented as the wheel of fortune, which is also identified with the wheel of life in Tibetan Buddhism and the Rota Mundi of the Rosicrucians. This is a number of rise and fall, and your name will be known either for good or evil.

10 represents a new beginning on a higher plane. Pythagorus considered it the most sacred number. In Indian philosophy, 10 is the number of karma, virility, prophecy and magical powers. In the Tarot, the wheel is said to represent blind fate. It is the card of adventurers and explorers.

If this is a number of a business house, it indicates expansion and financial gains. It is a favourable number for politicians and those occupying high governmental positions. You must guard against treachery which may cause your downfall. You have to discipline yourself to attain power. Pride may prevent you from realizing your potential. In calculations of future events this is a fortunate number, indicating that your plans will be successfully carried out.

11 This is considered to be a mystic and ominous number by many western occultists, associated with bad omens and sinners. It gives a special sensitivity for feeling vibrations and seeing spirits. It is also a warning of hidden dangers. In the Kabala, it is represented as a clenched hand and a lion muzzled. You have to contend with great adversities. In the Tarot, it signifies imbalance, disorder and frustrated individual initiative. In Hindu tradition, it is associated with obstinacy, dymanism and revolution.

You should try to understand the word of God and act faithfully. You will encounter duality, conflict and internal struggle. Some numerologists consider this a number of violence, power and success in fearless adventures. If this number is in harmony with your date of birth, you will be successful in interior decoration, the hotel, petroleum and film industries, chemicals, art and publicity.

12 In the Kabala, the twelfth path is that of prophetic vision. In the Tarot, it is represented as the hanged man. He has no contact with the earth and has voluntarily withdrawn from its denser influences to live in a dream world where his spiritual power is tremendous.

12 is a number associated with trouble, changes, danger, charity, spiritualism and wisdom. It is also related to suffering and anxiety. You may have to sacrifice yourself for others. Impracticality, extreme sensitivity and unreciprocated love are indicated.

You may suffer paralysis or bad circulation. Success will achieved mostly in the latter part of your life. It is advisable to change the spelling of your name to avoid having to sacrifice yourself.

13 In the *Sepher Yetzirah*, the thirteenth path is that of unity and understanding the truth of spiritual knowledge. It is symbolized in the Tarot by a skeleton or Death reaping down men with a scythe. It is widely believed to be a number of ill fortune. It symbolizes death, upheaval and strife.

13 is also the number of regeneration, transformation and spiritualism. Kabalist masters believe that he who understands 13 is given the keys of power and dominion, which if wrongly used cause self-destruction. The Mexicans and the Yucatans consider 13 to be a sacred number.

This is not a negative number in love affairs. It is also associated with geniuses and explorers. You may lack trustworthy friends, but you will be successful in research, creative work, religion or occult sciences. You have special skills for tackling crisis situations. However, you should be prepared for the unknown or unexpected. This number opens up the way for spiritual advancement.

14 In the Tarot and Kabala, this is represented as Temperance, a transition from a lower to a higher state. In the *Sepher Yetzirah*, the fourteenth path is that of sanctity and preparation. You should meditate on universal life and harmony. You will succeed if your aims are pure and you work persistently. Good orators, politicians and diplomats often have this karmic compound number. It is a lucky number for speculatiion, stocks and travel. Writing, publishing and media-related matters are associated with it.

It is the number of both risk and gain, movement, revolution, and of everlasting sexuality. Changes in business bring gain. However, pessimistic thinking may cause loss of property or failure in business. You must not rely on others. If you act cautiously you can be fortunate in financial dealings.

This number is associated with love and devotion, but also with lust and gratification. If this number appears in future calculations, you must act with great prudence. You may face danger from natural elements.

15 This is a number of magic, mystery and witchcraft. It is also associated with good speakers and skill in the arts. You will have great success if you are in politics, but if there is 4 or 8 in your birth date you may have an accidental or violent death. In the Middle Ages, 15 was associated with the witches' sabbath. In the Tarot and Kabala, it indicates the most resounding success or the greatest failure. It also signals treachery, unscrupulousness and greed in financial affairs. It is said that at 15, vice opens up before man in its frightening reality. When associated with a good fate number it is very lucky and powerful, but if it is associated with 4 or 8, you may use magic and witchcraft to fulfil your desires. It is a number of sensuousness and strong personal magnetism. It is considered very fortunate for obtaining gifts, money or favours from others.

16 This is number of grave warning. In the Tarot, it is represented by a tower struck by lightning from which a crowned man is falling. It is also called the shattered citadel.

Ambition prevents you from finding the true balance between spirit and matter. There may be accidents or disappointments in love and marriage, and a strange fatality. Failure of your plans, expecially in love and marriage, is likely. Avoid wounded pride and rigid dogmatism. This number is associated with weakness, loss of health or reputation, accidents and explosions. You may undergo surgery, depression or a miscarriage. You have to suffer for being ambitious, undertaking risks and displaying anger. There will be destruction before reconstruction.

This is a favourable number for literary activities. In political life it indicates uncertainties. To reduce the negative aspect of this number, you have to renounce fame and find happiness in other ways.

17 This number is represented in the Tarot by the star of the Magi, an eight-pointed star of Venus. It signifies peace and love. In the *Sepher Yetzirah* the seventeenth path is that of realization and reward of the righteous.

This is a number of intuition, expression, clairvoyance, beauty and hope. You will rise above the trials that you face. Be careful in selecting friends and choose your partners carefully. Spiritual discipline will bring you success. This is a number of immortality and you will be remembered. This number gives inspiration to artists, astrologers, poets and musicians. It indicates idealism and occult protection. It is a fortunate number, provided it is not in association with 4 and 8.

18 This number indicates conflict between spiritualism and materialism. The occult symbol is a blood-stained path or twilight. 18 signifies treachery, deception and bad judgement. This number is associated with war, strife and quarrels. In the Tarot, it is represented by a moon from which drops of blood are falling. These drops are being drunk by a wolf and a hungry dog while a crab hastens to join them. This number indicates errors in judgement, lies, doubt and evil influences. It symbolizes endings that make way for new beginnings. It is a very bad number for any city or country as it indicates unrest and instability.

This number indicates troubles in your personal life. You may make money through unfair tactics, but you may be deceived by friends. You may face danger from natural forces. This is a good number for doctors, healers and lawyers. For those in the military services and politics, it is a good number if it vibrates well with the date of birth.

18 is a number of genius and insanity, black magic and nobility.

19 This is the most favourable of all karmic compound numbers and is symbolized the sun or the prince of heaven, which indicates victory and creativity. It is a number of honour, good fortune in love, power, fulfillment and happiness. Sometime it may indicate vanity and ego.

20 This is the number of the judgement or awakening. In the Tarot, it is represented as a winged angel sounding a trumpet while a man, woman and child rise from a tomb with their hands clasped in prayer. It denotes delays and obstacles to your plans, but these can be overcome by patience and spiritual doubts. You may suffer from an inferiority complex. There will be new plans or a call to action for some great cause or duty. In future calculations this number is associated with delays and obstacles.

21 You will achieve honours and victory. This number is called the crown of the Magi. In the Tarot, it is represented by a picture of the universe. Victory however will be achieved after long struggle. The number indicates artistic power. It promises success in undertakings. 21 is associated with truth, honour and hope. It is considered to be one of the most mystic numbers.

22 In the Tarot, this is represented by a good man blinded by the folly of others, with a knapsack of errors on his back being attacked by a tiger. It indicates that you may be a dreamer who wakes up only when

surrounded by danger. This number is associated with delusion or false judgement. It indicates restraint, accidents and catastrophes. It not a good number if it appears in calculations of the future.

23 This number is associated with success and receiving help from superiors. It is called the royal star of the lion. It indicates fame and eloquence. It is good number for communication, and brings opportunities for improvement and success when it appears in calculations of future events.

24 This is a good number, indicating gains from the opposite sex, those in high rank and through artistic means. It is a number of love, money and creativity. You will achieve happiness in love. Avoid self-indulgence and egotism in love and career matters as everything comes easily. Be careful of heights. It is a favourable number if it appears in connection with future events

25 You will achieve success after a lot of disappointments. This number gives you spiritual wisdom and strength, as well as mastery of the occult. You will have strong intuitions and prophetic dreams. It is not a material number. You must not be tempted by black magic. It is a fortunate number if it appears in connection with the future.

26 You will suffer losses through speculation, partnerships and bad unions. It is a good number for diplomacy and secret services. It makes you eloquent. Always try to follow your intuition. Loss due to burglars and law-breakers is indicated. If this number appears in future calculations, you must be very careful of the path you are treading.

27 This is represented by the sceptre. It is an excellent number, promising authority, power and fame. You have courage and the power to think and act independently. Your creative, especially literary, endeavours will be successful. You have a creative intellect and love for the arts, peace, beauty and justice. This is a number of karmic reward and it is fortunate if it appears in connection with future events.

28 This is a puzzling number full of contradictions. Through you have great promise, you may lose everything if you do not make provisions for the future. You may suffer a breach of trust, face opposition or be harassed by law agencies. You may have to begin again from scratch. This is not a good number if it appears as an indication of future events. It is advisable to change the spelling of your name to achieve a more fortunate number.

29 This number is associated with heartbreak, unreliable friends and deception by the opposite sex. It foreshadows tribulations and unexpected dangers, especially from water and heights. It is advisable to change your name to a more fortunate number. This is not a favourable number if it appears in connection with future events.

30 This is a mental number, one of thoughtful deduction and intellectual superiority. Success depends entirely upon your attitude as you are likely to choose to neglect all material things. This number is considered beneficial in theatre and script writing. You love children and animals. You will achieve great success if you use your talents well. However, you may also be disloyal and treacherous. This number is associated with surgery, chemistry and medicine.

31 The vibrations of this number are similar to 30. You may be lonely and self-contained. You may show genius or great intelligence, but you may suddenly abandon everything for mental peace. It is not a fortunate number for material things.

32 This number is called the politician's vibration. It is a magical number associated with people and nations. You will be eloquent and have a magical ability to sway the masses. You should follow your own ideas and opinions as you may suffer losses due to others. You will have many friends. You are versatile and can master foreign languages. However, you may be immoral and lack spirituality. This is a favourable number in connection with future events.

33 This number carries the same vibration as 24. However, you will have greater financial success. It is favourable for more traditional businesses. Your relations with the opposite sex are harmonious and fortunate. You are dignified, considerate and discriminating. You may have unexpected gains through legacies and windfalls.

34 You will achieve success after many trials. This number is connected with advancement, research, religion, magic and philosophy. You will make gains through property deals or legacies. It is a fortunate number if it appears in connection with future events, marital relations and foreign trips. You should avoid speculation and risky ventures.

35 The vibrations of this number are the same as 26. You will inherit money and enjoy travel. However, ease may make you indolent. This number indicates advancement. But you must guard against treachery.

Avoid speculation and gambling. Women must follow their own intuitions in personal relationships. This is a favourable number for short-term relationships, but not for marital or domestic happiness.

36 This has the same vibrations as 27. It is a favourable number which brings power and success if you use your talent well. Though there may be delays, you will be successful. Guard against accidents. It is a fortunate number if it occurs in future predictions.

37 This number is associated with fortunate friendships and love. You will be successful in your professional life and gain through association with the opposite sex. You will benefit from working in partnerships. This is a fortunate number if it appears in calculations of future events.

38 This number has the same vibrations as 29. It is a very powerful spiritual number. It increases harmony, but if there is discord, it brings falsehood. This number indicates power and success if you use your talents well and are sympathetic to others. It may also cause misunderstanding.

39 This number has the same vibration as 30. It gives health, friendship and love. You are capable of rising to the greatest heights as well as sinking to the lowest depths.

40 This number has the same vibrations as 31. You can achieve success in business or literary work. This is not a favourable number in marital relations. You are a good investor and possess mathematical talents. You may suffer from isolation and rebellion. Men may marry a second time.

41 This number has the same vibrations as 14. It is a favourable number, and you will get what you desire. But you must keep your passions under control and not act in haste.

42 This number has the same vibrations as 24. It indicates success in the arts, especially singing. The negative aspect of the number is that it is associated with treachery and may cause violent death.

43 This number is called the death point. It signifies revolution, upheaval, failure and destruction when it appears in connection with future events. It is concerned with military activities and indicates failure of your plans and risks from firearms. There is danger of war, but victory can be gained by positive action.

44 This number has the same vibrations as 26. It is associated with bravery and success in practical undertakings. However, if you are too ambitious or have too great a desire for fame, you may suffer personal losses. You may achieve glory in political and military pursuits, but you have to exercise self-control and know when to stop.

45 This number has the same vibrations as 27. It indicates an early marriage. You will punish the wicked, help the distressed and be prepared for emergencies. It is a fortunate number. Trust your own judgement if you want to succeed.

46 This number has the same vibrations as 37. You have high ideals. You should check your ambitions to ensure steady progress. You will have a successful love life. This number is associated with great inventors, scientists and idealists.

47 This number has same vibration as 39. There is possibility of danger from water. You should be wary of deceit and treachery. You have the ability to handle money and statistics, and will make a good banker. If it occurs in connection with future events, you must guard against professional rivals.

48 This number has same vibrations as 30. You will have a happy marriage and general success, especially in the arts, theatre and entertainment. You may also possess psychic and prophetic powers. Try to avoid overindulgence.

49 This number has the same vibrations as 31. If you respond to the higher aspect of this number, you will be a diplomat and spiritual. If you respond to baser aspect, you will have great hatred and insincerity.

50 This number has the same vibrations as 32. You will have great success in many occupations. You will be eloquent, powerful and possess leadership qualities. You will live a life of intense and constant activity. You have a magnetic personality. You may be a dispenser of law or a commander of forces, but this may make you dominating. You do not fear death. This is a fortunate number.

51 This number is called the royal star of the waterman and is very powerful. You will have sudden advancement in any undertaking. This is a military number. But you may have to face attempted assassinations.

52 This number has the same vibration as 43. You will be drawn to the higher things in life.

53 This number has the same vibration as 8. You are a go-getter, a good military person or detective. But if you succumb to the baser aspect of this number, you may resort to spying, blackmailing and misusing your powers.

54 This number has the same vibrations as 9. It gives you eloquence, wealth and good health.

55 This number has the same vibrations as 10. Its symbol the sword. It is a victorious number. You are a natural leader with a dominating personality, especially in religious or ethical areas. This is an important and magical number.

56 You are nervous and mentally restless. You may gain fortune and distinctions. You should not fritter away your advantages by pursuing unworthy ambitions.

57 You will have prosperity in business and good health. You have a pleasant personality and like socializing.

58 You are frank and affectionate, but fickle-minded. You should be a doctor or occultist.

59 You have speculative tendencies. You will benefit through involvement in maritime activities, stockbroking or travelling. You will be long-lived and you overcome obstacles. This number gives you immunity from danger.

60 You have a cheerful personality. The vibrations of this number are favourable for being a lawyer, advisor and healer.

61 You are fond of travelling and pleasure. You are sincere and calm, and have a well-balanced personality. You are good at controlling others.

62 This number has the same vibrations as 8. You are good at details, but may not be successful in large undertakings.

63 You are a born missionary and reformer, and are passionate about working for the cause of those who are suffering. However, you also have a tendency to drift and waste your time.

64 This number has the same vibrations at 20. You are a good observer, more suited to professional than commercial pursuits. You have an affinity for literary pursuits. You may remain single.

65 This number is represented as the royal star of the scorpion. You will have powerful patrons and a happy marriage. But you may also encounter dangers.

66 This number has the same vibrations as 12.

67 This number has the same vibrations as 13.

68 This number has the same vibrations as 14.

69 This number is represented by the crown of Mars. It is associated with fortune, honour and fame.

70 This number is very fortunate.

71 This is a powerful number but not fortunate. You will face problems in both worldly affairs and health.

72 This number does not have a distinct potency of its own. However, it is said to a number of angels and mercy.

73 This number signifies wisdom. It has the same vibrations as 10.

Can a Change in Name Alter Your Destiny?

To achieve success, the vibrations of your name should be harmonious with your destiny number. Thus, if the numerical value of your name is not in harmony with the destiny number, you may face obstacles and restrictions. In such cases, it is often advisable to change the spelling of your name so that it has more favourable vibrations and you can achieve success. There are examples of name change found in the Bible. Abram and Sarai changed their names to Abraham and Sarah when God promised them a child. H is related to child bearing. Saul of Tarsus' name was changed to Paul when he became a religious leader. S denotes individualism, whereas P indicates introspection and inner peace.

You should however consult an expert numerologist before you change the spelling of your name, as this can have extremely powerful effects on your life.

The most famous historical example of the disastrous effects of a name change is Napoleon. His surname was originally spelt as Buonaparte. Later, this was changed to

Bonaparte and this resulted in his downfall and destruction. This example has been discussed by numerologists like Sepharial in *The Numbers Book* (D.B. Taraporewala & Sons, 1986, p.80) and Montrose in *Numerology for Everyone* (Sagar, 1982, p.51).

N	A	P	O	L	E	O	N		B	U	O	N	A	P	A	R	T	E
5	1	8	7	3	5	7	5		2	6	7	5	1	8	1	2	4	5

Sum of vowels: 40
Sum of consonants: 42
Unreduced karmic compound number: 82
Reduced karmic compound number: 10

This number is associated with greatness and fame.

N	A	P	O	L	E	O	N		B	O	N	A	P	A	R	T	E
5	1	8	7	3	5	7	5		2	7	5	1	8	1	2	4	5

Sum of vowels: 34
Sum of consonants: 42
Unreduced karmic compound number: 76
Reduced karmic compound number: 13

This number implies grave warning, and is represented by Death cutting down men with a scythe.

Karmic Compound Numbers of Some Famous People

It is interesting to read what the karmic compound numbers of some famous people and places say about their destiny.

A	D	O	L	F		H	I	T	L	E	R
1	4	7	3	8		5	1	4	3	5	2

Unreduced karmic compound number: 43

H	E	R	M	A	N	N		G	O	E	R	I	N	G
5	5	2	4	1	5	5		3	7	5	2	1	5	3

Unreduced karmic compound number: 53
Reduced karmic compound number: 17

R	A	J	I	V		G	A	N	D	H	I
2	1	1	5	6		3	1	5	4	5	1

Unreduced karmic compound number: 34

B	E	N	I	T	O		M	U	S	S	O	L	I	N	I
2	5	5	1	4	7		4	6	3	3	7	3	1	5	1

Unreduced karmic compound number: 57
Reduced karmic compound number: 12

A	T	A	L		B	E	H	A	R	I		V	A	J	P	A	Y	E	E
1	4	1	3		2	5	5	1	2	1		6	1	1	8	1	1	5	5

Unreduced karmic compound number: 53
Reduced karmic compound number: 17

J	O	H	N		F		K	E	N	N	E	D	Y
1	7	5	5		8		2	5	5	5	5	4	1

Unreduced karmic compound number: 55
Reduced karmic compound number: 10

A	L	B	E	R	T		E	I	N	S	T	E	I	N
1	3	2	5	2	4		5	1	5	3	4	5	1	5

Unreduced karmic compound number: 46
Reduced karmic compound number: 10

I	N	D	I	R	A		G	A	N	D	H	I
1	5	4	1	2	1		3	1	5	4	5	1

Unreduced karmic compound number: 33
Reduced karmic compound number: 15

S	A	D	D	A	M		H	U	S	S	E	I	N
3	1	4	4	1	4		5	6	3	3	5	1	5

Unreduced karmic compound number: 46
Reduced karmic compound number: 10

M	A	H	A	T	M	A		G	A	N	D	H	I
4	1	5	1	4	4	1		3	1	5	4	5	1

Unreduced karmic compound number: 39
Reduced karmic compound number: 12

I	N	D	I	A
1	5	4	1	1

Unreduced karmic compound number: 12

K	A	S	H	M	I	R
2	1	3	5	4	1	2

Unreduced karmic compound number: 18

U	S	A
6	3	1

Unreduced karmic compound number: 10

Your Expression Number

Your expression number shows the sum of your natural capacities or talents. These are the tools with which you have to work in order to succeed. Your expression number also indicates your mental capacity and method of thinking. You should strive to achieve the goals indicated by this number.

Many people who have great potential are not able to fulfil this. Their power is wasted in doing other things demanded by external conditions. This happens because the individual is busy working in an entirely different direction from his core strength.

How to Calculate Your Expression Number

Convert all the letters of your name into numbers using the Pythagorean values given on p. 114. Add the sum of the full name and reduce it to a single digit. You should also add the vowels and consonants separately and get the values for these. This is because you may lose an 11 or 22 expression in the vowels or consonants.

M	A	T	A		H	A	R	I
4	1	2	1		8	1	9	9

Thus Mata Hari's expression number is the sum of these digits, which 35. Reduced to one digit, 3+5=8.

What Your Expression Number Indicates

1 You are independent, ambitious and headstrong with a tendency to be self-centred. Guard against selfishness and egotism. You do not like to be directed. You put your original and creative ideas into operation quickly and efficiently. Strength and perseverance are essential to your success. People are either attracted or repelled by your personality. You have great powers of concentration and can visualize your goals. Do not be stubborn. Try to cultivate balance and compassion.

Though you may be a good starter, you are a poor finisher. You identify yourself so powerfully with your goals that you refuse to see flaws in your plans. External events limit and frustrate you. You may become so obstinate that you will not be diverted from a course of action which you know may be disastrous.

You must learn to exercise your individuality through understanding, not by control. You are an inventor and thinker, interested in new ideas. Professions you will be successful in are in the arts, politics, law and investment.

2 You are harmonious, imaginative and artistic. You dislike arguments and believe in peaceful coexistence. You are tactful and diplomatic, a natural peacemaker or arbitrator. You are romantic, faithful and affectionate. You also expect reciprocity from loved ones.

You are moody and sensitive, and get easily wounded by criticism. Your abilities are enhanced when working with others. However, you may be frustrated since you do not get recognition despite helping others. Your highly developed intuition will help you to judge people and gauge situations. You will do best as a psychologist, accountant, medium, interior decorator, artist, writer, teacher, judge, diplomat or in the arts.

3 You are ambitious, expressive and hard-working. Your keen dislike of working in subordinate positions will propel you to the top. You are a born entertainer with the gift of communication. Your verbal skills can draw you into theatre, music or writing. Try to make the best of your artistic abilities.

You need to guard against scattering your talents, as you lack discipline. Learn to concentrate and focus. Do not avoid responsibility and commitment, or be sarcastic and cynical. You like to bring joy to people. Your charming and cheerful nature makes you popular. The occult and unknown interest you.

In times of trouble, people will appear out of nowhere to help you. You are very loyal, generous, and loving in relationships. However, once you realize that relationship has ended, you do not look back. You are outspoken and can flare up easily. You will do well as a politician, lecturer, musician, lawyer, publisher, writer, singer, fashion designer, advertiser or real estate broker.

4 You are a builder and organizer, and know how to get things together. You thrive on hard work and routine. You are conservative and good with finances. You are tenacious and precise, and like to deal with things systematically. You dislike the unconventional.

You have a tendency to suffer from bouts of depression when you are overworked, and to be rigid and stubborn. Try to be more understanding of others' shortcomings. With patience, determination and honesty, you will be able to achieve much. You will do best as an accountant, scientist, economist, computer professional, builder, technician, mathematician, chemist or architect.

5 You love freedom and are interested in trying anything that is new, exciting and unusual. You are

characterized by magnetism, versatility and restlessness. You will be popular with both sexes. Your great talent lies in coping with the unexpected. You have an inquisitive mind and need to know why things are what they are.

Though you are a quick thinker, you can be disorganized. Try to be focussed and grounded if you want to achieve success. There is a tendency to give up a project before completion, as you get bored. You are lucky and can bounce back from any difficulty. Avoid being critical and sarcastic.

Though you are loving and affectionate, you are not constant in relationships. You have a great elasticity of character, so failures will not greatly affect you. Overindulgence in sensual pleasures can cause problems. Professions suitable for you are as an editor, lecturer, stockbroker, travel agent, detective, actor, critic or in public relations.

6 You are a logical and fair thinker with the ability to judge the right from wrong and to maintain order. Harmony in domestic life is essential for your happiness. You are responsible and trustworthy, and have a high regard for justice and honesty. You are a natural counsellor and healer.

You are however unable to integrate contradictions within yourself. As you are creative, you will be often drawn to the arts as a means of self-expression. You are romantically inclined, but your attitude towards relationships is idealistic. You enjoy entertaining. You may be accused of meddling in the affairs of other people. You are best suited to be an artist, doctor, interior decorator, musician, architect, singer, teacher, writer or welfare worker.

7 You are creative and imaginative, and deeply interested in all aspects of religion, mysticism and the

occult. Though you have great wisdom, you often have difficulty in expressing it. You will always be a mystery to others. You are given to meditation and contemplation. You have the ability to think abstractly and visualize the future.

It is your destiny to search for truth in spiritual or scientific fields. You may feel lonely even when surrounded by people. However, you need your own space. You will be loved and respected for your knowledge and philosophical insights. You can be very moody, and must take care to distinguish between real and imaginary fears. You have a strong dislike for the ignorant, mundane and superficial. This makes you critical and cynical. You resent injustice and may forgive but do not forget.

Your logical and analytical mind helps you to solve problems. You are a perfectionist. You may not be understood or appreciated, which may cause frustration. You are able to work best in an individual capacity. You may have artistic ability. Learn to communicate with other people. Professions suitable for you are as a psychologist, researcher, secret agent, musician, historian, actor, healer, artist, lawyer, scientist, astronomer or teacher.

8 You have the ability to work patiently and build. You have business acumen and can achieve prosperity, power and fame. You may experience great loneliness, but you will achieve success commensurate to your efforts and fulfil your goals. You may have to face sorrows and losses. You may also become greedy and ruthless.

You need proof of love and have great difficulty in expressing your affection. As an employer you are fair and just. Try to lead by your strength. You may reach great heights as an executive or in government. Try to balance the spiritual and the material. Professions in which you will achieve success are as a banker, lawyer, politician, scientist, executive, manufacturer, financial adviser, organizer or public servant.

9 You are a true humanitarian, capable of great spiritual and mental achievement. A born fighter, you do not tolerate injustice. You are impulsive and accident-prone. Your devotion to your loved ones can make you sacrifice everything for them. However, guard against letting the heart rule the head. You are ambitious and may make many enemies. You cannot tolerate injustice and discrimination. Love, romance, music and art will deeply interest you.

As you are compassionate and understanding, you will be very popular. You have an abundance of artistic talent. You will do best as a journalist, politician, spiritual leader, surgeon, musician, artist, union leader or in the media, the arts or the army.

Your Soul Urge Number

Pythagoras believed that numbers respond to particular wavelengths in the cosmos and these in turn produce tangible results. Some attribute the instant likes or dislikes we feel to such vibrations.

The vowels in the names are responsible for two people being attracted or repelled. The addition of the value of all the vowels in your name according the Pythagorean table (see p. 114) give your soul urge number. This is also known as the heart's desire number or ambition number. It reveals your natural talents, secret ambitions or ideals, and your self-opinion.

As stated before, the difference between the values of the consonants and vowels in your name should be minimal. The vowels reflect your mental state.

Friends and Marriage

If the value of someone's whole name is the same as that of the vowels in your name, that person will be greatly attached to you. If she/he has nothing in her/his name to answer your vowels, it will be you who will be doing all the giving.

There is excellent cooperation between two people when the values of their names are the same. Their minds are on the same plane. They make good business associates and friends.

When you and your spouse have the same value of

vowels in your names, you share common tastes and enjoy each other's company. The danger is that you may be so self-satisfied and content that your growth gets stunted.

The happiest marriage is one where your destiny number matches your spouse's soul urge number.

There is a close connection between your soul urge number and your spouse's soul urge number, fate number or destiny number. If any of these match with your soul urge number, there is harmony between you.

Have you ever wondered about the relationship of Adolf Hitler and Eva Braun? Hitler was born on 20 April 1889. His fate number is thus 2 and his destiny number 5. The value of vowels in his name is 21, thus his soul urge number is 3. Braun was born on 6 February 1912. Thus her fate number is 6 and her destiny number 3. The vowels in her name add up to 10, so her soul urge number is 1. His soul urge number is the same as her destiny number, indicating that theirs was a harmonious relationship.

Have you wondered if Bill Clinton and Monica Lewinsky could have had a future together had circumstances been otherwise? His birth date is 19 August 1946. His fate number is 1 and his destiny number is 2. The vowels in his name add up to 24, thus his soul urge number is 6. Her date of birth is 23 July 1973. Thus her fate number is 5 and her destiny number is also 5. The value of vowels in her name is 30, therefore her soul urge number is 3. As the soul urge and destiny numbers do not match, they were clearly not meant to be together.

What Your Soul Urge Number Indicates

1 You want to be the leader in everything that you do. You are extremely confident of your own abilities and possess the confidence to lead others. You cannot work in subordinate positions. Your keen insight enables you to evaluate the abilities of others. Remarkable will power

coupled with a strong desire to succeed enables you to achieve your goals.

You have a tendency to dominate others. You function independently, and should do work which allows you freedom. You should control your critical and impatient nature.

You like to handle grand plans. You must learn to delegate the details for others to finish. Ambition is your greatest motivating force. You need to develop kindliness and broad-mindedness.

2 Peace and harmony are important to you. You are a sensitive and emotional person, and you dislike confrontation. You are cooperative and adaptable by nature. Though you are tactful and diplomatic, you need to be more assertive.

You have a strong love for music and the arts. If 6 is prominent in your chart, you may have a good voice too. Learn to trust your intuition. You are very popular with friends due to your natural tendency to be a peacemaker.

On the negative side, you lack a definite purpose in life. Though you constantly accumulate wisdom, you do not have the motivation to carry out plans. You are not a good disciplinarian. You should develop your spiritual side.

3 You have a happy, friendly and outgoing disposition. You are the life and soul of any party. You have a good mental and emotional balance, coupled with the ability to inspire and entertain people. You express yourself well and you are drawn to acting, singing and writing. You must make a conscious effort to ensure that your creative faculties find proper outlets.

Fame and recognition motivate you. You are fond of children and pets. Your aesthetic sense is well-developed. Beautiful surroundings give you solace. You need to develop patience and concentration to maximize the wonderful talents with which you are endowed.

4 You are a very practical and result-oriented person. You like system and order in all things. You dislike frequent changes and are comfortable with routine. You wish to achieve honour and acclaim. You love honesty, loyalty and dependability.

You desire material power and tend to be a workaholic. Your analytical, thrifty and conscientious nature ensures success. You greatly desire to be loved but your rigid and stubborn nature keeps people away. You should develop a more flexible approach if you desire harmony and balance. Your conservative nature prevents you from accepting new ideas. You need to give more freedom to your family members who may feel that you carry discipline too far.

5 You are very versatile and original. Your love of change and desire for new experiences make you travel a lot. You have a sharp mind and a flexible nature, and can be involved in several projects simultaneously. However, you are sometimes unable to complete projects in hand.

You are highly enthusiastic person, easily excited about new ideas. You are sociable and attractive to the opposite sex. You must guard against the tendency to speculate. You should develop more concentration. Sex is important to you, but be careful of overindulgence.

6 Service and loyalty are very important to you, as are family and relationships. You are a good parent, teacher or counsellor. You make a very loyal and forgiving friend. You empathize with people and offer them help and support. You champion the cause of the downtrodden, but you must be careful because people may try to take advantage of this.

You enjoy working with people. You may possess artistic talent. Though you are very affectionate and caring, you need appreciation in return. You have a strong sense of justice. You are a perfectionist and expect similarly high standards from others. Keep away from negative people. You must guard against becoming too emotional, self-sacrificing, stubborn or argumentative.

7 You are a perfectionist in all things, and study and analyse things in depth. You base your theories upon scientific facts. You dislike manual labour in any form.

You prefer solitude to think and meditate. You are inclined to resent suggestions from others. As you are an introvert, you do not have a large circle of friends. You are seldom understood by others. You are idealistic and have great expectations from yourself. You are capable of great scientific or religious achievements. You must learn to be alone but not lonely. You need to share your emotions with someone close to you.

8 You desire power, success and material comforts. You possess leadership qualities and like to be at the helm of affairs. Your natural inclination is towards business and maintaining commercial fair play.

You must avoid being too exacting, dominating and stubborn. You have the tact and vision for commercial success. You must learn organization and cooperation. As you are logical and clear-sighted in your aims, you can take ruthless decisions.

9 You derive immense satisfaction from service to the community. You are highly intuitive, and your first impressions are often right. However, you are very impatient with those who cannot decide quickly.

You are a dreamer, interested in spiritual knowledge. You make a natural teacher, counsellor or healer. Your impulsive nature makes you take a lot of risks. Though you are very sensitive, you may sometimes lack understanding. You must learn to socialize, and use your knowledge for the benefit of others. Your forgiving and compassionate nature compensates for your other shortcomings. You can do well as an actor, writer or photographer.

Your Plane of Expression

By converting your name into numbers using the Pythagorean values (see p. 114), you can determine your temperament and the plane of expression in which you are strongest. There are four different planes of expression. These are:

The Physical Plane: This indicates involvement with physical adventures, creature comforts, order and material concerns. You will be good at physical and practical work.

The Mental Plane: This represents the mind, reason, analytical and executive ability. Your goals are well thought out and you have a logical attitude. You are suited for intellectual work.

The Emotional Plane: This involves the heart, imagination and creativity. You have an artistic nature and a willingness to serve others. Many musicians, artists, theatre persons, designers and philosophers are strong on the emotional plane.

The Intuitive Plane: This represents the psyche and the spiritual aspect. A majority of letters on this plane indicates great powers of intuition. You should work in occult or religious fields.

Plane	Numbers	Letters
Physical	4, 5	E, D, M, N, V, W
Mental	1, 8	A, H, J, Q, S, Z
Emotional	2, 3, 6	B, C, F, K, L, O, F, T, X, U
Intuitive	7, 9	G, I, P, R, Y

A combination of letters on the physical and mental plane means that you will be successful in the business world. A dominance of letters on the emotional and intuitive planes indicates that you should be in the arts. If you have a large number of letters on the emotional plane but more on the mental plane, you will be successful in medicine, law, marketing or human resources development. With more numbers on the emotional plane but a large number on the mental plane, you will be a good doctor, healer, author or successful in the arts and advertising.

What the Letters and Numbers Indicate

D, M, V	good intellect, dutiful, enjoyment of work or study
N, E, W	versatility, active, charm
A, J, S	creativity, initiative, independence
H, Q, Z	financial success if energy used wisely
B, K, T	tact and diplomacy
C, L, U	artistic or humanitarian leanings
F, O, X	best teachers and parents
G, P, Y	wisdom, perfection, authority
I, R	artistic and healing skills
More odd numbers	emotional, rebels against routine and discipline, artistic or humanitarian expression
More even numbers	practical, methodical, logical, able to give creative ideas shape

Thus, if your name is Ajoy Kumar, your temperament and plane of existence can be worked out thus:

A	J	O	Y		K	U	M	A	R
1	1	6	7		2	3	4	1	9

There are three letters on the emotional plane (K, U, O), three on the mental plane (A, J, A), two on the intuitive plane (Y, R) and one on the physical plane. Thus Ajoy is strong on the mental-emotional planes. He will be successful in medicine, law, marketing and human resources. The two letters on the intuitive plane indicate that Ajoy relies on his intuition in taking important decisions.

Your Intensification Number

In every name, the Pythagorean values of letters are usually repeated. There should be an average repetition of numbers in the name. Your intensification numbers indicates the talents you possess and the things you enjoy doing.

If any number is repeated too frequently, the character of that number will intensify certain aspects of your personality. Absence of any numbers indicates a flaw in your personality which may however be compensated by other digits of your birth chart. If a particular number is very prominent in a name, this should be treated as an important source of strength.

Numerologists who believe in karma state that missing numbers in your name reveal experiences that you avoided or acts of omission in the past. They state that this missing number is your karma number. Two individuals with the same fate number and destiny number may behave differently due to the different intensification numbers.

To use the example from the previous chapter, the numerical value of Ajoy Kumar's name according to the Pythagorean values is thus:

A	J	O	Y		K	U	M	A	R
1	1	6	7		2	3	4	1	9

The frequency of repetition of the digits is thus:

Digits	1	2	3	4	5	6	7	8	9
Frequency	3	1	1	1	0	1	1	0	1

1 is repeated thrice in the name, more than any other number. Thus Ajoy Kumar's intensification number is 1. 5 and 8 are missing in his name. These indicate flaws in his personality which need to be corrected.

What Your Intensification Number Indicates

1 Few 1s or the absence of 1 in your name indicates lack of self-confidence, ambition and decision-making ability. If you have only one or two 1s in your name, you lack independence and initiative. You are cooperative and not egotistical. More than three 1s in your name makes you original, strong-willed and inflexible. You should channelize your energy productively. More than four 1s in your name make you domineering and selfish, and can cause health problems, especially weakness of the head and lungs.

2 Few 2s or the absence of 2 in your name indicates carelessness with details, inconsiderateness and lack of tact. Impatience with family and colleagues may cause misunderstandings. More than two 2s in your name makes you cooperative and tactful. You shall be considerate, sensitive and a good analyst. Love of music is also indicated.

3 Few 3s or an absence of 3 in your name makes you impatient and inarticulate. You may waste your energy and have an inferiority complex. Try to focus on one idea at a time. If you have more than three 3s in your name, you are excellent in self-expression, writing or

acting. Guard against being impatient and irresponsible.

4 Few 4s or the absence of 4 in your name indicates dislike of hard work. You lack concentration and are impatient. You have rigid concepts of right and wrong. If you have three or more 4s in your name, you are hard-working and practical, and are a stickler for detail and order. You have good powers of concentration. However, you may be stubborn.

5 Few 5s or the absence of 5s in your name makes you lethargic and unwilling to accept change. You need to develop understanding and adaptability. Do not alienate those you love. More than four 5s in your name makes you versatile, resourceful and free-spirited. You have an attraction for the opposite sex. You love change, travel and excitement. Guard against being impulsive.

6 Few 6s or the absence of 6 in your name makes you irresponsible. Do not run away from love. Many 6s in your name indicates reliability. You will make a good teacher and parent and have humanitarian qualities. However, you may also have a tendency to be dominating and argumentative.

7 Few 7s or the absence of 7 in your name makes you unreasonable and lacking in understanding, analysis and spiritual sensitivity. You need to build your confidence by developing knowledge. You may have false pride which prevents you from knowing the metaphysical side of life. Many 7s in your name will make you a perfectionist, demanding proof and analysis. You have considerable scientific, technical or mathematical gifts and will achieve much. You are inclined to be reserved, secretive and introspective. You have an interest in the spiritual.

8 Few 8s or the absence of 8 in your name shows lack of materialism, and an inability to organize and manage. You must learn to value money and not depend on others. Two or more 8s in your name indicates good executive and business ability. You are good at organization and leadership, and will be successful in financial matters. Tact, a sense of justice and practical judgment are your other strengths.

9 Few 9s or the absence of 9 in your name makes you intolerant, selfish and narrow-minded. One 9 in your name makes you unsympathetic. Try to respect the views of others. More than four 9s in your name indicates a humanitarian and generous nature. You have artistic and literary abilities. You are kind and sympathetic to others. However, you lack practicality and are very moody. You have good intuition and enjoy travelling.

What Different Combinations of Numbers Indicate

Many 1s and 3s	Artistic talent and leadership talents
Many 1s and 4s	Originality and constructiveness
Many 1s and 6s	Humanitarian concerns
Many 1s and 7s	Research and analytical skills
Many 1s and 8s	Organizational skills
Many 1s and 9s	Originality in art and philosophy
Many 2s and 6s	Artistic talent and humanitarian concerns
Many 3s and 5s	Inspitation and freedom-loving
Many 3s and 8s	Artistic and philosophic talents
Many 2s or 3s and 9s	Artistic and spiritual talents
Many 4s and 5s	Practicality, hard-work and resourcefulness
Many 4s and 7s	Mathematical and scientific talents
Many 4s and 8s	Obstinacy
Many 6s and 7s	Artistic talent
Many 7s and 9s	Literary, philosophical and spiritual talents

Your Name Cycle and Event Number

The influence of your first name, middle name (if any) and surname operate on your life separately and simultaneously. To know your past, present and future from your name, you have to add the numerical value of the letters of each name according to the Pythagorean values (see p. 114) separately. You can read your future by seeing the influence of the individual letters in a given year (name cycle) as well as by combining the numerical value of the letters of your names influential in that year (event number).

Name Cycle: The numerical value of the name of Amitabh Mukherjee is given below.

A	M	I	T	A	B	H		M	U	K	H	E	R	J	E	E
1	4	9	2	1	2	8		4	3	2	8	5	9	1	5	5

The total value of Amitabh's first name is 27, and that of his surname is 42.

The numerological value of a letter represents the number of years the influence of that letter will last. For example, if he is transitting the letter M, the influence of this letter will last four years as the value of M is 4.

Amitabh's first-name cycle ends in his twenty-seventh year as 27 is the total of his first name. In his twenty-eighth year, his second first-name cycle will begin, which will continue until his fifty-fourth year. In his twenty-eighth year, he will be under the influence of A (first letter of his first name) and end in his fifty-fourth year with H (last letter of his first name). The third first-name cycle will begin in his fifty-fifth year.

The same formula will also apply to his surname cycles. The first cycle will end in his forty-second year and the second cycle will then begin.

Thus, for the first forty years of his life, these are the letters that will influence Amitabh's life. (The top line in the chart indicates the year, the second line the first name, and the third line the surname.)

1	2	3	4	5	6	7	8	9	10	11	12	13	14	15	16	17	18	19	20
A	M	M	M	M	I	I	I	I	I	I	I	I	I	T	T	A	B	B	H
M	M	M	M	Ü	U	U	K	K	H	H	H	H	H	H	H	H	E	E	E

21	22	23	24	25	26	27	28	29	30	31	32	33	34	35	36	37	38	39	40
H	H	H	H	H	H	A	M	M	M	M	I	I	I	I	I	I	I	I	I
E	E	R	R	R	R	R	R	R	R	J	E	E	E	E	E	E	E	E	E

Another system of interpretation is that of the yearly transit. You live one year in the vibration of each letter of your name. One complete cycle is completed when you transit your full name.

In this system, the influences working on Amitabh during the first forty years of his life will be as follows:

1	2	3	4	5	6	7	8	9	10	11	12	13	14	15	16	17	18	19	20
A	M	I	T	A	B	H	M	U	K	H	E	R	J	E	E	A	M	I	T

21	22	23	24	25	26	27	28	29	30	31	32	33	34	35	36	37	38	39	40
A	B	H	M	U	K	H	E	R	J	E	E	A	M	I	T	A	B	H	M

The years when the last letter of your first name and surname are influential are considered to be critical years, especially for old people. As Amitabh has sixteen letters in his name, he will be completing name cycles when he is sixteen, thirty-two, forty-eight and so on.

If your name is in harmony with your destiny number, it will ease difficult letter transits. The transit of letters operates from birthday to birthday, and not according to the calendar year.

Some numerologists call the transit of the first name the physical transit, the middle name the mental transit and the last name the spiritual transit.

Event Number: The addition of the numerical values of all three transit letters of your full name in any particular year reveals the event number for that year.

If Amitabh Mukherjee's middle name is Benoy, then his chart will look like this:

1	2	3	4	5	6	7	8	9	10	11	12	13	14	15	16	17	18	19	20
A	M	M	M	M	I	I	I	I	I	I	I	I	I	T	T	A	B	B	H
B	B	E	E	E	E	E	N	N	N	N	N	O	O	O	O	O	O	Y	Y
M	M	M	M	U	U	U	K	K	H	H	H	H	H	H	H	H	E	E	E

21	22	23	24	25	26	27	28	29	30	31	32	33	34	35	36	37	38	39	40
H	H	H	H	H	H	H	A	M	M	M	M	I	I	I	I	I	I	I	I
Y	Y	Y	Y	Y	B	B	E	E	E	E	E	N	N	N	N	N	O	O	O
E	E	R	R	R	R	R	R	R	R	R	J	E	E	E	E	E	E	E	E

Thus in his twelfth year, the letters influencing Amitabh will be I, N and H, which have the numeric values of 9, 5 and 8 according to the Pythagorean table (see p. 114). Thus his event number will be the sum of these, which is 22. As 22 is a master number, he must look at the influence of both the reduced and unreduced event number. Reduced to one digit, this comes to 4.

What Your Event Number Indicates

1 A new phase of your life is beginning, in which your will power will be tested to the limit. The situation will demand that you face difficulties head on. There will be many changes, new ideas and interests. There will be struggles, but you have to persevere. You will make new friends and develop new contacts. You may make changes in your profession or receive new responsibilities in your old one. You have to discard inefficient ways of working and relationships. You will be receive due rewards, and your knowledge, self-respect and self-esteem will grow.

Unreduced number 19: You will have a strong desire to break away from existing circumstances. You must think logically and control your strong desire for change.

Unreduced number 28: Avoid being egotistical and greedy.

2 This phase revolves around partnerships and alliances. Everything depends upon your ability to work with others. Delays can cause frustration. Adopt a flexible attitude. Trust your intuition as your perceptive powers will aid you. Do not force your judgments on others. You may be very sensitive and easily hurt. Take care of your health, especially the nervous system. Rest in harmonious surroundings, be positive-minded and avoid depression. You will be rewarded in partnerships and group activities if you exercise patience and cooperation.

3 This is a period of heightened creativity and your ability to express yourself will be at its peak. There will also be opportunities to express your talents. You may develop a serious hobby into a profession. You will make advancements professionally. There will also be social activities and travel. You will develop new friendships and romantic relationships. Do not scatter your energy in

frivolous pursuits. Maintain an optimistic and enthusiastic attitude. You will have mood swings so you must discipline yourself.

Unreduced number 12: There will be creative development through favourable associations.

Unreduced number 21: You may lose opportunities because of emotional rather than logical decisions.

4 You need to complete a lot of work in this phase. You have to work hard, but the reward will be proportionate. You have to plan your finances carefully. Work will increase and you will have heavy demands on your time. But any neglect will lead to problems. You may feel impatient at restrictions and slow progress. Your business or investment may expand or you may buy property. Your family will demand attention. You need to take care of your health.

Unreduced number 13: You will face many restrictions. Review personal opinions and make choices carefully.

5 This will be a very eventful period, marked by unexpected developments. You should take advantage of opportunities to develop your talents. Your business will flourish and expand. Unusual events will bring favourable changes and career advancements. You must always be alert to opportunities. Be disciplined and focussed on your long-term goals. You may have opportunities to travel. You will have immense personal growth. Avoid overindulgence in food, alcohol, sex and drugs.

Unreduced number 14: It may be very difficult for you to make the right choices despite many opportunities. Impulsive decisions due to selfish interests may create problems.

6 Family, love and marriage dominate this period. You will be expected to accept responsibilities and looked to for guidance and support. This is an emotional period. Your family may be demanding. Avoid acting harshly. There may be a substantial inheritance. You will form new and lasting friendships. Divorce may also take place. Career and financial matters will prosper. Selfless service will secure social recognition. Your artistic talents will be enhanced.

7 A steady period of introspection, meditation and search for inner peace. You will want to spend time with yourself and understand the deeper meaning of life. Your sensitivity and intuition will be heightened. This period is one of much thinking, study and understanding. You will be occupied with scientific, philosophical or metaphysical subjects. There may be experiences which lead to an inner awakening. This period is not favourable for love and relationships. You may damage close friendships unnecessarily, and there may be problems in your marriage. Do not make any drastic changes and think carefully before taking any major decisions. Relations with influential people will be formed. This is a period of self-discovery, and rediscovery of old pastimes.

Unreduced number 16: Things may not work out as you planned. There may be many unexpected events. This is a time for reflection and to develop faith. You will grasp opportunities which will bring unusual gains. You may experience frustration and humiliation due to your own behaviour.

8 This is a period of responsibilities and professional affairs. If you work hard, organize well and use your judgment rightly, you will gain power and recognition.

You will make a lot of money, but expenses will also be high. There may be a rise in profession or financial status. However, you may also make major mistakes. Travel for professional reasons is also indicated. You will have to settle old debts. There will be opportunities to make a new start. You must be alert in all your dealings. In matters of love, there may be problems. Buying and selling of property is also possible. Consistent efforts will make you influential.

Unreduced number 17: You will achieve success in some unusual line of business.

Unreduced number 26: Beware of treachery or wrong judgement of partners. You may suffer severe losses.

Unreduced number 35: There may be progress and financial gain.

9 You should take a broad view of life. If you live selfishly, you will suffer. You have to dedicate yourself to higher causes and contribute to society. There will be many opportunities for you in divergent fields, such as religion, business and art. You will be successful only if you work impersonally. This is a good period for travelling, achieving material comforts and making money. You may encounter legal problems if you are dishonest. Your ideals will be tested, but you will experience spiritual and psychological expansion. Love and friendship will be very important for you. You may have to terminate an important relationship, but this will eventually benefit you. You need to develop forgiveness.

Unreduced number 18: You need to cultivate tolerance and compassion to succeed.

11 This is a significant period. There may be failures on the material plane, but there will be many gains on the spiritual plane. Relationships and partnerships may end suddenly. Problems and misunderstandings may arise in both personal and professional life. This is a time for self-examination. You should follow spiritual pursuits to achieve new awareness and inner growth.

22 This is a significant period. There will be great demands and opportunities. You may be at the centre of some social movement. You need to work selflessly and honestly to avoid humiliation and disappointment. However, avoid excessive work. You will gain recognition and power.

What Your Transit Letters Indicate

A This is a period of change and new beginnings. You must seek activity which demands individual effort. Travel is also indicated, or a change of residence. This is the year for being independent, creative and inventive. You must protect your lungs.

B This letter indicates love affairs or marriage. Being too emotional or rigid may create problems in your relationships. This is also a good year for partnerships. You must be careful of problems of the nervous system. You will be successful in research and accumulation of knowledge. This letter brings peace, happiness and prosperity.

C There will be much socializing. You may have an impulsive love affair. Though you will be very optimistic, guard against self-indulgence and extravagance. You may have premonitions or psychic experiences. You will be more eloquent and expressive. This will be a happy and carefree year full of activity.

D This year is good for making investments and saving. You have to work hard, and be economical and practical. There will be a lot of opportunities for growth. Diet and eating habits need attention. Travelling is also indicated. Your love life will improve if you share your thoughts and feelings. You will develop good friendships. You must control your temper.

E This is an intuitive letter and you must not ignore your hunches. Your learning skills will be enhanced. There may be many changes in career, residence and relationship. You will be attracted to religion and philosophy. Be careful in legal matters. There will be much travelling and social activity. Your finances may fluctuate. You will be nervous and uncertain, so try to be firm. Take care of your liver and guard against gallstones.

F Financial conditions may improve this year. You have to pay attention domestic affairs. Love and marriage will bring restrictions. This is a time for introspection. You have to make many adjustments and compromises, but do not avoid responsibility. It is a good time to do humanitarian services. If you have a selfish attitude, you may suffer in both domestic and professional life. You must guard against ear and heart trouble.

G This is a contradictory period. The vibrations of the year are on the mental plane. This is good time for study, research, meditation and spiritual enrichment. Financially, this is a good time. You may have a tendency to brood and be depressed. Be careful of deceit and betrayal. In emotional matters you will be inclined to be impulsive.

H This is a good year for growth in business and finances. But you need to discipline yourself, and guard against quarrels and misunderstandings. You need love and attention, and are emotionally vulnerable. You may travel for professional purposes and write. Professional interests take precedence over domestic ones. Do not overexert yourself. You may suffer from mental strain.

I The emphasis will be on emotional and romantic matters. There may be marital troubles. You may experience restrictions on both professional and personal fronts. Try to be calm and tolerant, do not slip into depression. Be careful as you will be prone to accidents. Financially, this is a good period. You need to guard against stomach problems.

J This is a good year for starting anything new. You need to be a leader. Though financial vibrations are good, you may vacillate and leave things unfinished. You may change your career and residence. If there are two Js or J and S in combination, you may not select the right opportunities. You must guard your lungs.

K This is a good vibration for business, growth and meeting new people. You will have clear vision and intuition. Fame and fortune may come your way. Guard against treachery and dishonesty. You will be frank in speech and expression. It is a good time for spiritual growth. You may have strange psychic experiences. Sudden love affairs and friendships may begin. You must guard against nervous strain.

L This letter indicates intuition and mental development. This is good year for making new friends and socializing. There will be many pleasure trips, love and marriage. Creative pursuits are favoured. You must also strive for spiritual insight. Guard against problems with your throat and voice.

MThis letter has a materialistic vibration. This will be a rather subdued year. Your energy levels may not be high. You need to work hard and be practical. Financial rewards will be slow but are assured. You may have to make sacrifices in a relationship as your partner will be demanding. You may suffer from problems related to blood.

NThis is the period to exercise your imagination. You will expand your horizons and have adventures. This will be a rewarding period in your professional life. Many changes can take place, including residence. You may forge important social contacts which may benefit you in the future. You will be impulsive and feel sensual, and there will be fluctuations in your finances. Take care of your health, follow a fitness regime and develop a positive attitude.

OYour finances will improve and there will be many opportunities. This is a good time to study, and religion and spirituality attract you. Your leadership skills will develop and come to the fore. Avoid living negatively and being egotistical. You may have some troubles in marriage. Strong emotional experiences are indicated. You may have problems of the heart and liver. If O and X occur together, additional responsibilities will cause discomfort and frustration. If two Os occur together, these frustrations will be enhanced.

PThe vibrations of this year are mental. There will be disappointments in relationships. Many unexpected events will occur and you will not be in full control of the situation. Your talents will be recognized and rewarded. You may experience problems in love and marriage. You will be successful in teaching or writing. You must focus on spiritual growth. Do not speculate or take unnecessary risks.

QThis will be a peculiar and uncertain year. Your intuitive powers are greatly enhanced. Guard against impulsive decisions. You will attract or get attracted to unusual people. A major change in your work environment may take place. You will travel for professional reasons. Your love life takes a back seat. Business will flourish. You may suffer from digestive problems.

RThis will be a positive period with many opportunities and much growth. Your creative faculties will develop and you will gain money and power. Be careful in whatever you do. There will be confusion on the emotional front, and the domestic situation may be difficult. You must develop tact and wisdom.

SThis will be an emotional year. You must ensure that emotions do not hinder logical thought processes. There will be sudden changes in all spheres. There may be an awakening of hidden aspects of your personality. This is a good period for dealing in real estate. Guard your lungs.

TThis will be an emotional year. You may take recourse to meditation, yoga and solitude. Spiritualism will strongly attract you. There may be a change of residence. You will fall in love easily. You must guard against headaches.

UThis will be a receptive year attracting peculiar vibrations and experiences. Old emotional issues may crop up again. Control your emotions as they can interfere with opportunities and cause domestic problems. You will hear from people who have not been in touch for a long time. This is a creative period with many enjoyable experiences. You will become interested in metaphysical subjects. You may suffer from duality of the mind and lack confidence. Guard your throat. If you have two Us together, there will be emotional confusion due to intense feelings.

VThis letter has a powerful mystical and spiritual vibrations. Your intuitive faculties will get enhanced. You will be lucky in money matters, but you will also be extravagant. There will be promising opportunities in business. Important ventures will be started and there may be outstanding development. Your personal power will grow. Use tact and wisdom. Guard against nervous tension.

WYou need to accept the verdict of fate. Do not hold on to unpleasant experiences which occured in the past. This is an adventurous period when many changes will take place. You will aim high but may lack the energy to see your plans through. Self-discipline is essential to achieve growth. Do not live in the world of the senses. Legal problems may worry you, but things may well turn out in your favour. There will be unexpected happenings, and ups and downs. Guard against liver disorders.

XThis will be a year of constant emotional adjustments and turmoil. You may be involved in secret liaisons and escapades, leading to problems. If you work unselfishly, you may be rewarded by public recognition. There may be problems between parents and children.

You will search for peace, but it will remain elusive. This is called the letter of crucification. Spirituality and service can help to alleviate problems. Avoid unconventional people and ideas if you desire peace.

Y This will be a strongly perceptive and intuitive year. You will experience varied spiritual or psychic phenomenon. Meditation and spiritual pursuits will be beneficial. Love, marriage and partnerships may suffer due your tendency to be aloof. Avoid stimulants and spicy food, and follow a fitness regime. This year is more favourable to pursuing mystical interests than finances.

Z This will be a period of enormous progress and success. You will successfully handle emotional crises. Financial prospects appear bright. There will be unusual domestic conditions. You may develop a new relationship, bringing many changes including residence. Unusual friendships, love affairs and marriage are indicated. This is a good year for writers. You may suffer from stomach problems.

Using Numbers

Your Health Indications

USING YOUR NAME

Your name can give vital clues about your health. This can be done in two ways.

The initial letter of your name and its Kabala value according to Sepharial (see p. 115) can be used to interpret health indications. This corresponds to the indications given by your ascendant star in your horoscope.

Alternatively, the value of the whole name can be worked out, using according to its Kabala value. The total value of the name is reduced only if it exceeds 22. The whole name corresponds to the planetary vibration which exerts a constant influence on your life.

To work out the health indication for Suchita Singh, the first letter of her first name, which is S and has a value of 21, can be used. Alternatively, the full Kabala value can be worked out.

S	U	C	H	I	T	A		S	I	N	G	H
21	6	11	8	10	22	1		21	10	14	3	8

The total Kabala value of her first name is 139. When the digits are added, the total comes to 13. The total Kabala value of her surname is 56. When the digits are added, the total comes to 11. Thus the Kabala value of her whole name is the sum of the two totals, which is 24. As the value exceeds 22, which is the highest Kabala value, the total has to be reduced. Reduced to one digit, the

Kabala value of her whole name is 6.

What Your Health Number Indicates

1 This has a positive influence on your health as long as you do not succumb to stress and worry. You must maintain an optimistic attitude. Long walks and travel, especially in the countryside, will help to reduce your anxiety and restlessness.

2 This number rules over the digestive and excretory tracts. You must take immediate remedial action if any sluggishness is noticed. Be very careful with your diet and avoid eating out too frequently. You may suffer from colic, diarrhoea, constipation or enteric fever.

3 This number gives you a well-formed body with good recuperative powers. This number rules over the lumbar region, kidneys and skin. Emotional and mental disturbances affect you strongly. You must curtail your sugar intake as you may suffer from aliments caused by excess sugar. You shall also be prone to kidney disorders, urinary complaints, uraemia, jaundice and stones. You may also suffer from colds in the nose and head.

4 This number rules over the uterus, bladder, excretory system and pelvic region. You can maintain good health if you have regular habits. You have good physical strength and endurance. You may suffer from appendicitis, hernia and stones. You must exercise discretion in sexual encounters, and take precautions against infections. You may be prone to fevers.

5 This is a favourable numbers for health. You have a good appetite, but you must be careful of your caloric intake. Watch out for boils, abscesses and malfunctioning

of the liver. Be careful where food and drink are concerned. You will have good recuperative powers, but there will periods of illness.

6 This is a favourable number for health. Your well-being is greatly dependent on harmony in surroundings and personal relationships. Emotional tension affects you as much as physical illness. You have good recuperative powers and your body is in good condition. You must be careful about your kidneys and eyes.

7 You have a strong constitution and good recuperative powers. You may have bad health due to overactivity or mental and emotional strain. In later years, there will be a tendency to high blood pressure. This number governs the hips, eyes, liver and lungs. You may suffer from ailments related to these organs. You must take adequate physical and mental rest and control your restlessness. Danger through travel, sports and animals is indicated. You need to watch the condition of blood as impurities will cause boils and abscesses.

8 Your health condition will improve as you grow older. In youth you will be delicate. This number governs the joints and skin. You may suffer ailments of these parts, from falls, colds, chills, rheumatic pains, catarrh and asthma. You need to be careful of your digestive and eliminatary tracts.

9 This number governs the legs, ankles and eyes. Though you have a strong body, you need to maintain purity of blood. You must prevent sluggishness of circulation which could lead to poisoning of the blood and have adverse effects on the heart. You will be susceptible to colds and chills. You must not overexert yourself. You may have a tendency to varicose veins, leg or ankle troubles, and injuries through falls or accidents.

10 The condition of your health depends entirely on your nervous system which gets easily affected. Your digestive system gets upset by worry, tension and loss of sleep. You must not take risks while travelling or mountain-climbing as this number is associated with illnesses due to shock or accidents.

11 This number has a mixed effect on health. It is a psychic number. As your imagination is powerful, ailments may be self-induced, and psychological or emotional in nature. You should be careful of food poisoning, excessive use of medication and drugs, and smoking.

12 You do not have a strong constitution. You must guard against colds and chills, which affect the lungs and respiratory organs. You must take care of your diet to preserve good health. Try to avoid eating tinned food and beverages containing lime. Maintain good hygiene, and be careful of your liver and feet. You will live long.

13 You will have a strong constitution and vitality, as long as you take reasonable care of yourself. Your health may be affected by mental or physical overactivity. If you are ill, your natural restlessness will intensify, causing insomnia. You must guard against physical strain caused by hasty actions. You may be susceptible to influenza.

14 You have a strong constitution, great endurance and resistance to disease. You have a good appetite but this could lead to weight problems in middle age. This

number governs the throat, neck, tonsils, vocal chords, ears, cerebellum and eyes. Good health can be maintained by avoiding extremes and exercising discretion in food and drink.

15 This is not a favourable number for health. You may suffer from injuries affecting your bones, weak knees, rheumatic pains, colds and vitamin or mineral deficiencies. These can be largely remedied by healthy food habits. This number promises longevity. If proper care is taken, your health will improve in the latter part of your life.

16 Your health will be fairly good. You will have a strong and muscular constitution. You are prone to cuts and wounds, especially on the hands and face. You are liable to suffer from fever, especially while travelling or residing in hot climates. This number accentuates risk-taking which can lead to accidents. Always be careful when handling machinery and instruments.

17 You have a strong constitution, but are negatively affected by mental strain caused by disharmony in your personal and professional life. You must avoid mental or physical overactivity. You are also susceptible to asthma, bronchitis, nervous disorders, pleurisy and other lung troubles.

18 This number indicates a long life but does not give you a robust constitution. Your digestive system gets easily affected by worries and wrong diet. This number governs the stomach, abdominal region, sternum and chest. You may be susceptible to digestive and gastric troubles, dry coughs and chest congestion.

19 You have a strong constitution. This number governs the spine, back, heart and blood. You may suffer from complaints related to these organs and fevers. Though you have good recuperative powers, you suffer enormously when ill. You must avoid being unduly excited or overactive as this may have adverse effects on the heart.

20 This number governs the stomach and abdominal region. In women, it rules over the breasts and womb. Women may suffer from gynaecological problems. Personal hygiene is important to maintain good health. You may suffer from digestive problems due to wrong diet and a sensitive stomach. This number ensures longevity.

21 This number indicates good health and vitality. You may be susceptible to infections in youth. Regular exercise will help you to preserve good health. Your health will remain good until the age of sixty, but after that you need to be careful. You must avoid overexertion or excitement which may affect the condition of the heart.

22 Your health depends upon the season you were born in. Guard against colds and keep warm if you were born in winter. If you were born in autumn, your marital life and personal relations have a major influence on your health. If you are not happy, your health will suffer. If you were born in spring you need to develop self-control to regulate physical and mental restlessness. If you were born in summer, you will be prone to outbursts of temper, which will be harmful to your health. But your health will generally be good and will improve in the latter part of your life.

USING YOUR FATE NUMBER

What Your Fate Number Indicates

1 This indicates a strong constitution. But you may suffer from palpitation or irregular blood circulation. You should massage the body with almond or sesame oil to maintain good circulation. You may have trouble with your eyes, especially astigmatism. Your temperament is bile-dominated, therefore you must avoid oily food, meats and fish. Avoid eating in the late hours of the evening. You may suffer from high blood pressure as you grow older. You also suffer from over-exposure to the sun and heat.

Much of your physical weaknesses can be attributed to negative emotions. A positive attitude can easily negate the ill effects. You must take care of the lower back and spine. Eat foods that purify the blood. Avoid eating bitter, acidic and dry substances. Fasting on Sundays and a salt-free diet are beneficial.

The months in which you are vulnerable to ill health and overwork are October, November, December and January. Foods which you should eat frequently are oranges, lemons, dates, raisins, barley and barley bread. Saffron, St John's wort, cloves, nutmeg, sorrel, borrage, gentian root, lavender, bay leaves, thyme and myrrh are also beneficial to you.

2 You have a tendency to suffer from stress which upsets your nervous system. You are also perpetually bothered by stomach and digestive problems, so be careful of what you eat. Gastric trouble and internal growths may also occur. Men may suffer from sexual problems and women may suffer from uterine troubles and teucorrhea. Your chest may be also vulnerable. Most problems are caused by anxiety. The months which you are vulnerable to overwork and ill health are January, February and July.

Foods which you should frequently consume are lettuce, melon, cucumber, turnips and cabbages. Chicory, linseed, rapeseed and endive will also benefit you.

3 Avoid consumption of oily substances. Consume plenty of liquids to avoid gall bladder problems. You should be careful of problems related to blood. You may suffer from overstrain of the nervous system due to overwork and lack of sleep. You are prone to attacks of sciatica, neuritis and skin problems. You may also be susceptible to liver, thigh and hip problems, arthritis and jaundice.

December, February, June and September are the months which you must guard against ill health or overwork. Foods you should frequently consume are cherries, beetroot, gooseberries, mulberries, peaches, olives, rhubarbs, pomegranate, pineapples, grapes, apples, figs, hazelnuts and strawberries. Dandelion, sage, mint, saffron, nutmeg, cloves, St John's wort, borage and sweet marjoram are also beneficial.

4 You should have only vegetarian food and abstain from alcohol. You may suffer from strange ailments which are difficult to diagnose. You may suffer melancholy, anaemia, mental disorders, poor circulation and pains in the head and back. You must have orange seeds and fenugreek seeds to protect you from heart troubles, blood pressure and strengthen the immune system. Carrot juice, beet juice and fruit juice must be regularly taken to build up your haemoglobin count. Consume herbal teas, sprouts and leafy green vegetables. Your physical weaknesses get aggravated by negative emotions. Be careful of injuries to the lower leg. You will benefit from hypnosis and mental suggestions.

January, February, July, August and September are the months in which you must guard against ill health and overwork. You should eat spinach regularly. Sage, Solomon's seal, medlar and pilewort are good for you.

5 You are vulnerable to nervous breakdowns caused by attempting too much and depleting your energy resources. Insomnia is a frequent problem. You suffer from pains in the shoulders and arms, and twitching in the face or eyes. You tend to get easily excited and become irritable under the slightest mental tension. You must try to control your emotions. Avoid being rude to elders. Try to discipline your mind through yoga or meditation. Sleep and peaceful surroundings have a healing effect on you. You may also suffer from skin ailments, headaches and indigestion.

June, September and December are the months in which you should guard against ill health and overwork. Foods which you must consume frequently are carrots, oatmeal breads, parsley, parsnips, walnuts, hazelnuts and other nuts. Sweet marjoram, caraway seeds, thyme and champignon are beneficial.

6 You have a strong constitutions, but you should live in the countryside or where you can have plenty of fresh air and exercise. You should pay attention to your weight, maintain a simple diet and avoid overeating. You suffer from congestion and infections of the throat, nose and lungs. Women often suffer from breast problems. You are emotional and suffer from weak nerves. You are extremely sensual and may suffer from depletion of energies due to overindulgence. You are also vulnerable to bladder, kidney and urinary problems. In later years, you may suffer from irregular circulation.

May, October and November are the months in which you must guard against ill health and overwork. Foods which you must frequently consume are apples, peaches, apricots, melons, spinach, beans, parsnips, figs, walnuts and almonds. Pomegranates, musk, violets, vervain, rose leaves, mint and motherwort will improve your health.

7 Worry is your biggest enemy. Most of your worries are imaginary. You are very sensitive to your surroundings. You should avoid solitude as well as the company of those who disturb your peace of mind. Your problems are usually caused by overwork. Your skin is very sensitive, especially to sunlight and friction. Try to avoid hot and spicy foods as you are prone to acidity. Include cereals in your daily diet, and eat onions and other vegetables containing sulphur. You are also be susceptible to gout and arthritis. Avoid smoking and drugs, and consume plenty of fruit juices and vitamins D and E. Long walks in the countryside are beneficial.

January, February, July and August are the months in which you should guard against ill health and distraction. Foods you should consume frequently are lettuce, cabbage, mushrooms, cucumbers, apples, cranberries and fruit juices. Chicory, linseed, sorrel and colewort are good for you.

8 You are prone to rheumatism, gout, depression, colic pains and ear troubles. Your liver, intestines and the excretory system may also cause problems. You have a tendency to develop migraine and headaches. You should avoid animal foods. You should also increase the iron, vitamins A, D and E, and calcium in your diet as you may suffer from anaemia and impurities of the blood. Massage will be beneficial. Depression is more commonly associated with this number than others.

January, February, July and December are the months in which you must guard against ill health. Foods which you should consume regularly are spinach, carrots, broccoli and celery. Sage, wintergreen, plantain, shepherd's purse, solomon's seal, vervain, elderflower, gravel root and mandrake root are good for you.

9 You are prone to suffer from varieties of fevers, chicken pox and measles. You have good recuperative powers. You will suffer from sudden illnesses but will not easily be affected by chronic illness. You must be careful as you are prone to accidents to the head, cuts and burns. Avoid alcohol and rich food. You should be careful of skin diseases, ulcers, and lung and nose infections. You may get infections by casual sexual activities. Avoid drugs, intoxicants, and hot and oily food. Morning walks and oil massages will be beneficial.

April, May, October and November are the months to guard against ill health and overwork. Foods you should consume frequently are garlic, onions, tomatoes and rhubarb. Mustard seed, white hellebore, ginger, pepper, rapeseed, hops, daneworth and nettle will improve your health.

Your Lucky Colours

You can choose your numerological colours to be your magnetic best. The right choice of colours leads to harmony of mind and body. You should choose colours that harmonize with your fate number, soul urge number, destiny number and expression number.

For parties and entertainment, you should wear the colours of your fate number. When you need to relax or protect yourself against adverse vibrations, you must wear the colour of your soul urge number. These colours can also be worn for success in love, romance and friendship. To attract new opportunities and professional success, wear the colours of your destiny number. These colours should be worn as often as possible. Wearing the colours which are in harmony with the vibration of the day will be beneficial in business matters. For enhancing your intellectual capabilities, you should wear the colour of your expression number. Some numerologists believe that wearing the colours of your destiny number improves your health. The colour of the day and the colour of your date of birth should be harmonized to create a magnetic centre attracting things with similar vibrations.

Numbers and colours are bound together in the law of vibrations. Numbers have relationships with planets, sound forms and colours.

Number	Colour	Planet	Sound
1, 4	orange	sun	A, I
6	blue	Venus	O, U, W
5	yellow	Mercury	E, H, N
7, 2	green	moon	B, P, F, V
3	violet	Jupiter	soft G, J, Ch
9	red	Mars	K, hard G, R
8	indigo	Saturn	D, S, Sh, Z

Colours have certain historical associations. Also, it has been scientifically proven that the body responds to different colours in very specific ways. Your personal choice of colours reveals much about your personality.

Black: This is traditionally associated with mourning and sorrow. It is also used to symbolize witchcraft and black magic. Christian artists use black to indicate Satan. People who wear a lot of this colour tend to be worldly, sober and dignified.

Red: This is associated with life and passion. It may also signify an excess of passion and bloodshed. The senses respond to this colour, and it is believed to speed up metabolic processes.

Red is associated with outgoing people who are assertive and energetic. The colour stimulates the senses and emotions.

Orange: This increases appetite and induces relaxation. This colour is associated with generous people with strong loyalties. It stimulates creativity and ambition.

Yellow: This is a sacred colour for the Chinese, Egyptians and Greeks. In India, it is considered auspicious. It is associated with warmth and wisdom. This colour is believed to increase stress. It is associated with shy people.

White: In ancient Rome, medieval France and in India, this is the colour of mourning. It is also associated with innocence and chastity.

Blue: This colour is associated with truth, tranquillity and fidelity. It signifies peace to Buddhists. This is believed to induce relaxation and tranquillity. People who like this colour are believed to be loyal and sensitive.

Green: This is regarded as sacred by Muslims and lucky by the Irish. Buddhist art uses it to indicate the permanence of life. It is associated with new life and spring. It also represents jealousy.

This colour is supposed to have healing properties. People who prefer this colour tend to be affectionate and sensitive.

Purple: In the west, this is the symbol of royalty. It is associated with mystery and wisdom. People who like this colour tend to be spiritual.

Brown: This symbolizes humility and strength. It reduces irritability and fatigue. People who wear a lot of brown tend to be dependable and stubborn.

Grey: This is associated with age and modesty.

Your Fate Number and Colours

You should wear the colours favourable for your fate number, and also use them in your workplace and home to work and relax better.

Fate number	Colours you should use
1	Brown, orange, copper, purple, yellow and gold.
2	Green, pale yellow, salmon, silver and white. Avoid black, purple and dark red.
3	Mauve, rose, violet and orange.
4	Blue, silver, grey and maroon. Avoid strong colours.
5	Light shades of grey, silver and pink in glistening shades. Avoid dark colours.
6	All shades of blue, earth tones, green and pink. Avoid red and cream unless you are an Aries or a Scorpio.
7	Pale green, purple, magenta, white, yellow and gold.
8	Dark shades of blue, purple, brown and black. Avoid light and gaudy colours.
9	Dark shades of red, crimson, pink, purple, blue and white.

Your Destiny Number, Your Expression Number and Soul Urge Number and Colour

Number	Colours you should use
1	Crimson and flame
2	Salmon and gold
3	Rose, gold and flame
4	Green, blue and indigo
5	Turquoise, lemon and pink
6	Scarlet, orange, wine and heliotrope
7	Purple, brick red, violet and lavender
8	Mauve, tan, yellow, canary and buff
9	Red, brown and lavender
11	White, black, yellow, violet, silver and dark green
22	Cream

Numbers in Your Daily Life

THE IMPORTANT YEARS OF YOUR LIFE

The important years in your life are those which are equal to the number of letters in your name and the sum of your birth date, in both reduced (which would be equal to your destiny number) and unreduced from, and multiples thereof.

Thus the important years in the life of Suchita Singh, born on 15 July 1961, would be

- Her twelfth year (the number of letters in her name)
- Her thirtieth year as the sum of her birth date is 30. 7+1+5+1+9+6+1=30. This is her major cycle.
- And multiples of the above two numbers.

Reduced to one digit, her birth date is 3 (3+0). Her inner or minor cycle is of three years' duration.

WHAT IS A GOOD DAY?

To find out whether a particular day is good for you, add your karmic compound number to your birthday. Add the day you want to check up. Then see the corresponding karmic compound number reading for this sum.

Thus, if your karmic compound number is 24, you are born on 10 August and you want to find out how 7 November is lucky for you, you have to add the following: 24+10+7=42

Then you should check what this karmic compound number signifies before scheduling any important event on this day.

YOUR LUCKY NUMBER

The day and time of your birth determines which your constant lucky numbers are. This hour and day shows the planetary influence. The corresponding numbers will recur in your life in a positive way.

In the ancient Hindu hora system, it is believed that the seven planets influence each hour of the day. The order in which they preside over the successive hours is determined by their distance from the earth. The days of the week are named after the planets. Some western numerologists count of the planetary hours from noon, the Hindu system counts the planetary hours from the first hour after sunrise. This is always presided by the planet ruling the day. As the time the sun rises changes, the first hour after sunrise will also vary. For the associations of the planets with numbers, see p. 11.

The Hindu day begins at sunrise and ends at sunrise the next day. Therefore, if you are born at 3.30 a.m. on Tuesday, 15 January according to the Roman calendar, then in the Hindu calendar, you are born in the twenty-second hour after sunrise (if sunrise was at 6.30 a.m.) on Monday, 14 January. Therefore you would have to consult the corresponding section of the chart below.

Hours after sunrise	1 8 15 22	2 9 16 23	3 10 17 24	4 11 18	5 12 19	6 13 20	7 14 21
Sunday	1	6	5	2	8	3	9
Monday	7	8	3	9	1	6	5
Tuesday	9	4	6	5	7	8	3
Wednesday	5	2	8	3	9	4	6
Thursday	3	9	1	6	5	2	8
Friday	6	5	7	8	3	9	1
Saturday	8	3	9	4	6	5	7

COMPATIBILITY CHARTS FOR RELATIONSHIPS

Based on Your Destiny Number

Excellent Compatibility

2	2	2	3	3	4	4	6	6	7	9
2	6	9	6	9	4	6	6	9	7	9

Good Compatibility

1	1	1	1	1	2	2	3	4	4	4	6	6
2	3	6	7	9	4	7	5	7	8	9	7	8

Medium Compatibility

1	1	2	2	3	3	4	5	5	5	5	6	6	7	8
1	8	3	8	4	7	5	6	7	8	9	7	8	8	9

Poor Compatibility

1	1	2	3	3	5
4	5	5	3	8	5

Destiny Number Harmonies

1	3, 5, 7
2	4, 8
3	1, 5, 6, 7, 8
4	2, 8
5	1, 3, 7
6	3, 9
7	1, 3, 5
8	2, 4
9	3, 6

Based on Your Birth Chart

You have to fill in your and your partner's dates of birth in the fixed squares.

Your date of birth is 28 November 1947 and your partner's is 25 April 1941.

		9
2		8
111	4	7

		9
2	5	
11	44	7

28 November 1947   25 April 1941

Mental compatibility is indicated by the fact that both of your have a single 9 on the intellectual plane. You both are extremely practical, as indicated by the strong numbers on the bottom row. You give your partner in 8 energy which she/he lacks and she/he gives you the 5 energy which you lack. Therefore both of you are able to complement the other.

Ideally, similarity on the mental plane ensures great understanding, and give and take of emotional and material digits means you are complementary. There may be disharmony if you and your partner have exactly the same digits or if you have exactly the same digits on any one plane. This is also true of business partnerships.

Another way of working out compatibility is by adding your unreduced soul urge numbers (value of the vowels in your name and your partner's names) and seeing the interpretation of the corresponding karmic compound value.

YOUR DATE OF BIRTH AND YOUR RELATIONSHIPS

Broken Engagement: You may have a broken engagement if you have 2, 8 or 9 as the third or fourth digit in your year of birth.

More Than One Marriage: You may marry more than once if you have the following combinations in your date of birth:

- More than one 2 or 7 if your destiny number is 3, 5, 6, 7 or 9.
- If your destiny number is 2, 4, 6, 8 or 9, and you have more than one number which is the same as the destiny number of your partner and in association with 7.

Divorce: Incidence of divorce is higher among people whose destiny number is 2 or 9. If you have 2 and 3 in your date of birth, especially in your year of birth and a third digit which is not favourable to your destiny number, the chances of divorce are higher.

Disappointments in Love: You may suffer disappointment in love if you have the following combinations in your date of birth:

- If you have 2 or 8, but do not have 5.
- If you have 7 but do not have 4.
- When your destiny number is antagonistic to 7, such as 2, 3, 4 or 8.

Unmarried: You may remain unmarried if you have any of the following in your date of birth:

- More than one 0 or 6.
- 1, 4, 5 or 7 are missing.

Widowhood: If your date of birth has 0 connected with the destiny number of your spouse, and 2, 5 or 8 in association with 7.

IS YOUR CITY FAVOURABLE TO YOU?

There will be opportunities for growth and development in the city if
- It has the same vibrations as your date of birth.
- The sum of the vowels in the name of the city is the same as the sum of vowels in your name.

There will be good professional opportunities in the city if
- It has the same expression number as your name.
- It has the same name vibration as your destiny number.

You should live in a town whose name total is the same as your birth month, according to Kabala theory.

The vowels of the name of a city or community are said to indicate the collective mind of the community. The consonants indicate the city's personality or the impression it makes on people.

If your vowels do not vibrate well with the town you live in, you should adopt a signature with vowels that harmonize with those of the town. However, it takes time to establish a name vibration, especially if you have used your earlier signature for a long time in business and legal affairs.

CHOOSING YOUR HOUSE NUMBER

The total of the house number should be in the same concord as your birthday. If the other members of your family belong to different concords, then you should choose a number that adds up to 6 as this number is associated with harmony and domesticity.

For your clubs and other places where you spend your

leisure hours, you should choose places where the name has numerological associations of peace and harmony.

TRACING LOST OBJECTS

This ancient Hindu system of divination tells you whether lost things can be found, and if they can be, then where. Divination is a science in that it involves calculation and interpretation. It is also an art as subconscious and automatic means may be used.

It was believed that numbers have a direct reference to things thought of. A particular thought form has a definite relation to a particular number. In this method, a certain spontaneity of mental action is required. The process should be as automatic as possible. Therefore, if a number is thought of immediately after a lost object is mentioned, this number would be a natural sequence to the thought form.

You must free your mind of all other matters and concentrate on the issue or object. Write down the series of nine digits between 1 and 9 that you think of. Add 3 to the sum of the nine digits. Then refer this sum to the question at hand.

For example, the numbers thought by you are 7, 5, 6, 3, 2, 1, 5, 6 and 7. The sum of numbers is 42. Now add 3 to this. The final sum will be 45. Check the indications given by 45.

1   Search in the living room or the master bedroom, near a white curtain. Ask a child, who may give a clue.

2   It will be found within the house, in or close to a vase or bowl. Take the help of your maidservant.

3   It is among books, between papers or in a passage.

4   It is not lost. It will be found in your possession.

5   It is not lost. Look under some headgear, under a cloak or garment, or on a hook for hanging clothes.

6   It is near the shoe rack, probably on a shelf, stand or rack.

7   Ask your maidservant. A woman has kept it while arranging the wardrobe.

8   It is on the top of a cupboard, shelf or some ledge. A servant or workman will find it.

9   It is in a child's clothing.

10 It is in the living room. You will get it back.

11 It is at some distance, not in the house. It likely to be near a tank, pool or body of water.

12 Search your workplace or where you keep books and papers. It is safe.

13 Search in the cloakroom or where you keep your shawls.

14 Recovery is doubtful. Try the washroom, lavatory, sewer or drain.

15 Ask your spouse. Check the stables or where the animals are kept.

16 There is a good chance of recovering it, ask your cook.

17 Check where you keep your valuables or works of art, perhaps on some shelf.

18 It is misplaced in the house. You will find it among clothes.

19 It is in a small passage or lane, a short distance away from the house.

20 It is not lost. You will find it by water or near some carpet or linen.

21 It is in your possession. It is in a trunk or a box which folds in two parts.

22 You will soon find it. It is on a shelf in the house.

23 Search your wardrobe, among dirty clothes or maybe a short distance away.

24 It is safe with you. You will soon find it.

25 Search your personal belongings. It is near something white and round.

26 Ask the oldest person the house. He has kept it safely.

27 Search where the animals are kept. Ask the chauffeur or look for it in the garage.

28 It is lost but will be found.

29 You will get it back. Ask your old servant who may give you a useful hint.

30 Ask the children. It has been lost in play.

31 Search in the bathroom, washing place or closet.

32 Look near the veranda, corridor, or near something oblong.

33 You will find it among your clothes or personal belongings.

34 It will soon be found. It is near a fire or by a fireplace.

35 Try the bathroom, near a washing stand or a secret spot near water.

36 Your servant will return it.

37 You will find it in a prayer room or private apartment.

38 You will get it back. You may need to make a short journey to a place of ablution used by you.

39 It is not lost but accidentally put on a shelf.

40 Someone has wrapped in your clothes, a turban, loincloth or other apparel.

41 Search near the shoe rack.

42   It is close to a water body, or in the house of the servant.

43   You will find it, perhaps in the garage or where the animals are kept.

44   It is near the oil containers or lamps. You will find it but it might need purifying.

45   It is on a shelf or cupboard. It is as good as found.

46   Your partner has put it in safe custody.

47   Two servants are working together. Ask them. It will found by questioning the one who is uneasy on the feet.

48   It is near the drinking water place.

49   It is virtually lost to you. Even if you find it, it will be in a very damaged condition.

50   It is in some box or trunk. You will find it.

51   Check the bathroom or lavatory. You will find it.

52   Ask the mistress of the house, your partner or some relatives. It has changed hands.

53   A male servant who is in possession of it will return it.

54   Search the children's room or the place where they play. It is within the family.

55   It is near a water draining place or where water is.

56   It is probably where you last stopped on your journey. Contact the people there and you will find it.

57   It is possibly in your sports equipment, in a saddle bag or a pocket. You have the article.

58   It is very difficult to recover it. Two people are in possession of it and may have converted it or tampered with it.

59   Question the old servant. It may be found in flour or

some powder required for cooking.

60 It is lost forever.

61 It is near the shoe rack or in the lower part of the house.

62 It will not be found.

63 It is among your personal belongings or in an old dark place.

64 Look in the dark corners, high places or the attics.

65 The chances of finding it are poor. It has gone out of your hands and you may need to employ an agent to recover it.

66 It is as good as lost. Two servants are involved in the theft.

67 You will find it. A young child will help you.

68 Ask your servant to fetch it from the top of the house or the terrace.

69 It is some distance away, perhaps where you last had been. It may be near the entrance of a relative's house.

70 It is near water. It will be found.

71 Search on the floor near your feet.

72 It is in your possession, close to a water pot or a tank.

73 Lodge a complaint with the police. You will recover it.

74 A faithful servant will get it back to you.

75 You will find it, but it will be in very damaged condition as it is in the hands of some youngsters.

76 It is where you keep cereals and foodstuff.

77 It is a short distance away. A servant will bring it to you.

78 It is as good as lost.

79 You have it. Search near the iron cupboard or other metal object.

80 It is in your possession, perhaps in a box, trunk or close to the shoe rack.

81 Search for it among clothes. If you are lucky, you may find it.

82 Look for it in the kitchen.

83 It is near a water tank or pool. A young girl will recover it for you.

84 It is in a box or case within the house.

PERIODICITY OF NUMBERS

Numbers recur regularly in certain patterns. Given below are some examples:

4, 8 and 9 and Recent Indian History

In Indian astrology it is believed that Uranus (4), Saturn (8) and Mars (9) are negative influences. It is interesting to note that many of the unhappy incidents in Indian history have occurred in years where the sum of the digits adds up to one of these three numbers.

1948 (4)   Assassination of Mahatma Gandhi
1962 (9)   Chinese aggression
1971 (9)   Bangladesh war
1975 (4)   Declaration of Emergency
1984 (4)   Operation Bluestar and assassination of Mrs Gandhi

2 and Kings

2 is an unfortunate number for European kings:

Charles II of France was poisoned.
Edward II of England was murdered.
Richard II of England was murdered.
Henry II of England was murdered.
Henery II of France killed in a tournament.
George II of England died suddenly.

0 and US Presidents

US presidents elected in a year ending with 0 usually die in office or face assassination attempts.

1880	Thomas Jefferson
1820	James Monroe
1840	William Henry Harrison
1860	Abraham Lincoln
1880	James Garfield
1900	William McKinley
1910	Theodore Roosevelt (assassination attempt)
1920	Warren Harding
1940	Franklin Roosevelt
1960	John F. Kennedy
1980	Ronald Reagan (assassination attempt)

Numerological Yantras

Magic squares were used in China over four thousand years ago. In India, there was a parallel science using mantras and yantras (geometrical designs) together with astrology and numerology.

Pythagorus believed that each planet had a distinctive sound which combined together to form the music of the spheres. This sound is described in the Vedas as aum, and called logos in the Bible and kalma-i-illahi in Islam. In ancient India, it was believed that certain sound frequencies and combinations had the power to stir up astral energies and utilize them for material purposes. Mantras are repetitions of such sounds, which when recited give rise to certain psychic energies which can be utilized to achieve your purposes.

Astro-numerical yantras are used for multiple purposes, such as attracting love or favours, and promoting prosperity. Some popular yantras found in the ancient Indian texts are given below. Most of these yantras are written on bhoj patra (bark of birch tree), using a peacock feather and asthagandha during the period of the waxing moon. After purification and recitation of mantras, the yantras are carved or embossed on copper, silver or steel plates.

There are certain auspicious times to make yantras. For securing the love of the beloved, the 10th to the 20th of the lunar month is auspicious, especially Mondays. For success in business, wealth and fulfilment, the yantra should be written on a Monday during the first ten days of the waxing moon.

To Create Love Between a Man and a Woman

4	9	2
3	5	7
8	1	6

This has to be drawn on a Friday in the hour of Venus.

To Reconcile Differences Between a Couple

4	15	3	5
9	6	3	16
7	12	13	2
14	1	6	11

11	8	1	14
2	13	12	7
16	3	6	9
8	10	15	4

This yantra should be worn around the neck by either of the two.

786

2	9	4
7	5	3
6	1	8

This has to be written on a Saturday in the hour of Saturn or Mars, or on Wednesday or Friday.

For Those Who Face Opposition in Love

14	7	9	4
1	12	6	15
8	13	3	10
11	2	16	5

Wearing this yantra ensures safe meetings away from the house.

Venus Talisman

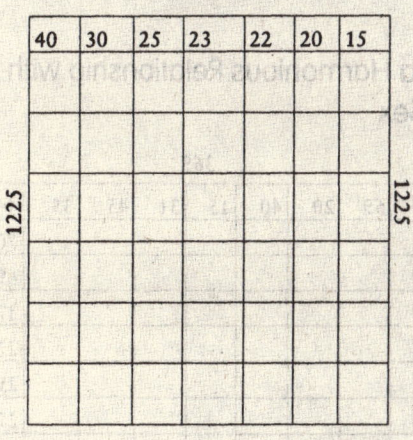

1225

40	30	25	23	22	20	15

1225

1225

1225

This yantra ensures love and respect from the opposite sex. It also gives you peace of mind. This has to be prepared in the phase of waxing moon on a Friday in the hour of Venus, Jupiter or the moon. It has to be worn or kept on yourself.

To Get the Man of Your Choice

786

24762	24768	24771	25320
24770	24758	24763	25341
24759	24773	24766	25325
24767	24761	24760	25344

The woman must drink the water of the washed yantra from a china plate. The yantra must be written with asthagandha.

To Create a Harmonious Relationship with the Opposite Sex

369

369								369
80	59	20	40	15	31	45	35	44
75								70
41								69
27								37
46								22
18								29
31								27
39								22
22								49

This is written and embossed or engraved on a Monday during the waxing moon. You can write it also on white paper or a silver plate. It is effective against the negative influence of Saturn.

To Find Missing Persons

62	69	2	6
6	3	68	65
68	63	8	1
4	5	64	67

Write this yantra on bhoj patra with asthagandha and hang it.

249	254	257	242
256	243	248	253
244	259	250	247
251	246	245	255

Write this with asthagandha and revolve it in the reverse direction on a spinning wheel.

For Success in Worldly Affairs

45

4	9	2
3	5	7
8	1	6

45

This is especially effective when Saturn causes problems for you during its seven-and-half-year transit over the natal moon.

Sun Yantra

6	7	2
1	5	9
8	3	4

This is engraved on a gold or copper disc or ring and worn on Sunday. It eliminates the negative effects of an afflicted sun.

Moon Yantra

7	8	3
2	6	10
9	4	5

This is engraved on a silver disc or ring on a Monday. It secures peace of mind and good friends.

Mars Yantra

8	9	4
3	7	11
10	5	6

This is engraved on a gold or copper disc or ring on a Tuesday. It gives protection from accidents, injuries and quarrels.

Mercury Yantra

9	10	5
4	8	12
11	6	18

This is engraved on a silver disc or ring on a Wednesday. It improves the memory.

Jupiter Yantra

10	11	6
5	9	13
12	7	8

This is engraved on a gold disc or ring on a Thursday. You will gain power and authority.

Venus Yantra

11	12	7
6	10	14
13	8	9

This is engraved on a silver disc or ring on a Friday. You will be attractive to the opposite sex.

Saturn Yantra

12	13	8
7	11	15
14	9	10

This is engraved on a steel disc or iron ring on a Saturday. It counters the evil effects of Saturn.

Rahu Yantra

13	14	9
8	12	16
15	10	11

This is engraved on paper with astha dhatu on a Thursday.

Ketu Yantra

14	15	10
9	13	17
16	11	12

This is engraved on paper with astha dhatu on a Thursday.

	Characteristics	Lucky Dates	Lucky Days	Friends	Lucky Colours	Romance
1	ambitious, determined, strong willed, tenacious, original	1, 19, 28	Sunday, Monday, Thursday	1, 3, 4, 6, 9	Yellow, gold, brown, orange, bronze	1, 3, 4, 6, 8
2	resourceful, adaptable, psychic, moderate, imaginative	2, 20, 29	Monday, Friday, Sunday	2, 4, 6	all shades of green cream white	2, 3, 7, 8
3	good mental abilities, independent confident, egotistical, dignified	3, 12, 21, 30	Thursday, Friday, Tuesday	1, 3, 6, 7, 8, 9	mauve, violet, purple	1, 3, 6, 9
4	logical, reliable, practical, materialistic, critical insight	4, 13, 22, 31	Sunday, Monday, Saturday	1, 2, 4, 7, 8	blues, grey, half tones, white	1, 4, 6, 8
5	adaptable, active, energetic, versatile, diplomatic	5, 14, 23	Wednesday, Friday	1, 3, 5, 7	light greys, white, green	3, 5, 6, 8
6	loving, sympathetic, intuitive, domestic, methodical	6, 15, 24	Tuesday, Thursday, Friday	1, 3, 6, 9	blue, rose, pink, turquoise	1, 2, 6, 8, 9
7	original, restless, idealistic, intense	7, 16, 25	Sunday, Monday, Thursday	3, 4, 7, 5, 9	white, yellow, pastel green, golden	2, 3, 7, 9
8	just, equitable, constant, methodical, industrious	8, 17, 26	Saturday, Monday	3, 4, 5, 8	dark grey, black, dark blue	1, 2, 4, 7
9	courageous, aggressive, rash, inventive, philosophical	9, 18, 27	Tuesday, Thursday, Friday	1, 3, 4, 6, 7, 9	red, rose, crimson, pink, white, purple	1, 3, 7, 9

RECKONER

Marriage	Lucky Gems	Business Partners	Health Problems	Professions	Important Years
1, 2, 4, 9	Amber, topaz, diamond	1, 4, 9	heart, eyes, BP, sunstroke	diplomat, politician, real estate, teacher, head of institution or industry	1, 10, 19, 28, 37, 46, 55, 64, 73
1, 2, 7, 8	moonstone, pearl jade	2, 7, 8	stress, nervous and digestive disorders	author, painter, artist, journalist, actor, scientist, preacher	2, 11, 20, 29, 38, 47, 56, 65, 74
3, 5, 6, 7, 9	amethyst	3, 5, 6, 7, 9	nervous strain, skin, liver	lawyer, administrator, teacher, banker, scholar	3, 12, 21, 30, 39, 47, 56, 66, 75
1, 4, 6, 8	Blue sapphire	1, 4, 6	depression, heart trouble, BP	astrologer, magician, businessman, transport, electrical engineer	4, 13, 22, 31, 40, 49, 58, 67
3, 5	diamond	3, 5, 9	skin, nervousness, insomnia	accounts, writing, radio, stockbroker, law, business	5, 14, 23, 32, 41, 50, 59, 68, 77
3, 6, 9	emerald, turquoise	3, 6, 9	ENT problems, lungs, breasts	healthcare, beauty, modelling, fashion designing, artist, writer, musician	6, 15, 24, 33, 42, 51, 60, 69, 78
2, 3, 6, 7	moonstone, pearl cat's eye	2, 3, 6, 7	acidity, gout skin, arthritis, excessive worry	teaching, journalism, films, exports, artist, medicine	7, 16, 25, 34, 43, 52, 61, 70, 79
1, 2, 4	amethyst, black pearl, black diamond, blue sapphire	1, 2, 8	rheumatism, teeth, colic pains, intestines	scientist, doctor, chemist, accountant, mining, civil servant	8, 17, 26, 35, 44, 53, 62, 71, 80
1, 3, 6, 9	garnet, ruby, bloodstone	1, 3, 6, 9	fevers, boils, bronchial or throat infections	army, doctor, banker, organizer	9, 18, 27, 36, 45, 54, 63, 74, 81

Bibliography

Adams, Mary, *Advanced Numerology* (D.B. Taraporewala & Sons, 1996)

Barratt, Rodford, *Numerology: An Introductory Guide to the Power of Numbers as a Guide for Life* (Element, 1990)

Basham, A.L., *A Cultural History of India* (OUP, 1975)

——, *The Wonder that Was India* (Rupa, 1967)

Chaudhri, Dr L.R., *Practical Remedial Measures* (Sagar, 1994)

——, *Practicals of Yantras* (Sagar, 1984)

Cheiro, *Book of Numbers* (Prentice Hall, 1988)

Choudhury, V.K., *The Impact of Ascending Signs* (Sagar, 1995)

Cross, Dr Unite, *Number Please* (Sagar, 1974)

Daruwala, Bejan, *Star Signs, Numerology, Chinese Astrology* (Jaico, 1991)

Dcoz, Hanz, *Numerology: A Complete Guide to Understanding and Using Your Numbers of Destiny* (Avery, 1998)

Encyclopaedia of Magic and Superstition (Octupus, 1974)

Frawly, David, *Astrology of the Seers* (Motilal Banarsidass, 1992)

Galedreyer, Ronnie, *Indian Astrology* (HarperCollins, 1990)

Goldschneider, Gary, *The Secret Language of Relationships* (Penguin, 1994)

Gray, Uma, and Gray, Marlow, *Numerology for Newlyweds* (St Martin's Press, 1997)

Hitchcock, Helen, *Your Number Please* (Sagar, 1973)

Jain, Manik Chand, *Birthday Numerology* (Sagar, 1974)

Johari, Harish, *Numerology, with Tantra, Ayurveda and Astrology* (Inner Traditions, 1990)

Kapoor, Dr Gouri Shankar, *Remedial Measures in Astrology* (Ranjan, 1995)

Katakkar, M., *Miracles in Numerology* (Jaico, 1990)

Kozinsky, Isadore, *Numbers: Their Meaning and Magic* (D.B. Taraporewala & Sons, 1940)

Kumar, Ravindra, *Secrets of Numerology* (Sterling, 1992)

Leigh, James, *How to Apply Numerology* (Sagar, date not given)

Leo, Allan, *How to Judge a Naturty* (Sagar, 1995)

——, *Practical Astrology* (D.B. Taraporewala & Sons, 1986)

Mazour, Anatole, and Peoples, John, *Men and Nations: A World History* (Harcourt, Brace and World Inc, 1960)

Montrose, *Numerology for Everyone* (Sagar, 1982)

Ojha, Ashutosh, *Numerology for All* (Orient Paperbacks, 1973)

Rice, Paul, and Rice, Valeta, *The Name Analysis Book* (Samuel Weiser, 1987)

Sander, C.G., *Practical Numerology for Everybody* (D.B. Taraporewala & Sons, 1996)

Scott, Ian, *The Luscher Colour Test* (Washington Square Press, 1969)

Sen, K.C., *Hast Samudrika Shastra* (D.B. Taraporewala & Sons, 1960)

Sepharial, *Kabalistic Astrology* (D.B. Taraporewala & Sons, 1986)

——, *Manual of Astrology, Palmistry and Occult Sciences* (D.B. Taraporewala & Sons, 1988)

——, *The Kabala of Numbers* (W. Foulsham & Co, 1928)

——, *The Numbers Book* (D.B. Taraporewala & Sons, 1986)

Shine, Norman, *Numerology: Your Character and Future Revealed in Numbers* (Atrium Press, 1995)

Showers, Paul, *Fortune Telling* (Sagar, 1973)

Shrimali, Narayan Dutt, *Numerology for Everyone* (Hind, 1992)

Simon, Sylvie, *The Tarot Art of Mysticism and Divination* (Cresent, 1991)

Taylor, Ariel Yvonne, *Numerology Made Plain* (Newcastle Publishing Company, 1973)

Tulli, Mahan Vir, *Numbers and Your Fortune* (Sagar, date not given)

Vega, Phyllis, *Numerology for Baby Names* (Dell, 1988)

Walker, Dr Morton, *The Power of Colour* (B. Jain, 1995)

Walton, Dr Roy Page, *Dates and Numbers: What They Mean to You* (D.B. Taraporewala & Sons, 1986)

Webster, Richard, *Chinese Numerology* (Llewellyn, 1998)

——, *Numerology Magic* (Llewellyn, 1998)

Westcott, W. Wynn, *Numbers: Their Occult and Mystic Powers* (D.B. Taraporewala & Sons, 1994)

Feng Shui Made Easy

Richard Webster

Feng shui is an ancient Chinese prescription for successful and harmonious living. By simply rearranging your furtniture, hanging windchimes outside, or placing a vase filled with flowers in your bedroom, you can affect the universal force called ch'i—the powerful magnetic energy that attracts good luck and prosperity.

A dose of feng shui every day will bring you health, wealth and happiness in many ways. *Feng Shui Made Easy* is an easy-to-follow and practical guide that can help you attain everything you desire: get the promotion, smooth out family quarrels, sleep soundly at night, and have more energy.

- Learn why successful people practise the art of feng shui.
- Discover why your home may be draining you of health, happiness and wealth.
- Get rid of the 'shars' in your living environment—straight lines and sharp angles that produce bad luck, misfortune, even disasters!

For thousands of years, the art of feng shui has helped people bring harmony into their homes and work environments. If you finally want life to go your way, try feng shui now!

Siddha Medicine
A Handbook of Traditional Remedies

Dr Paul Joseph Thottam

The Siddha system of medicine is believed to have orginated during the days of the Indus Valley civlization and continues to be popular today, especially in south India. It uses a fascinating combination of herbs, oils, minerals and massage therapy to promote good health and longevity.

Drawing on his collection of ancient manuscripts and years of practice, Dr Thottam writes this lucid account of the basic precepts of the system. In the first section of the book, he enumerates the different branches of Siddha medicine and explains their underlying principles, such as the panchamahabhuta and the three pinis, as well as the diagnostic procedures and the unique methods of preparing and using medicines. The second part outlines the basic formulas, cures for common diseases, and different kinds of massages and yoga.

This handy and helpful handbook will be a valuable reference for practitioners and a useful introduction for those interested in alternative systems of medicine.

Light on Life

Hart deFouw and Robert Svaboda

Jyotish or Indian astrology is an ancient and complex method of exploring the nature of time and space and its effect upon the individual. Formerly a closed book to the West, the subject has now been clarified and explained by Hart deFouw and Robert Svaboda, two experts and long-term practioners. In *Light on Life* they have created a complete and thorough handbook that can be appreciated and understood by those with very little knowledge of astrology.

Jyotish states that by considering the state of the cosmos when an event occurs, we can begin to understand its nature—and to prepare an appropriate response. Although there are similarities with Western astrology, there are also profound differences. Jyotish is, above all, infused with the religious, psychological and physical spirit of India. This comprehensive and enlightening book on the subject will prove a necessity to every astrologer or student of Indian thought.

The Penguin Guide to Vaastu

Sashikala Ananth

Almost fifteen hundred years before modern architecture came into its own, *Vaastu Shastra*, the classical Indian treatise on architecture, had set down principles of good planning and design which have been in practice in this country every since.

Today, people expect a Vaastu application to provide them instant cures and unending prosperity by relocating an entrance, window or room. However, Ananth, in this meticulously researched book, seeks to place Vaastu in its proper perspective as a highly evolved science, ridding it of the myths surrounding it. She examines the schools of thought existing in the tradition, the system's application, and the responsibilities of the designer.

Supplemented with beautiful illustrations, this book is an authoritative text which combines traditional wisdom with the needs of a modern and transitional society.

Home Remedies
(Volumes I, II and III)

T.V. Sairam

'Years of research on ancient Indian herblore by T.V. Sairam is slowly but surely taking the shape of easy-to-use volumes on the medicinal values of the phenomenal wealth this country has in herbs ...'

—*The Hindu*

The result of three decades of extensive research and meticulous documentation, the three volumes of *Home Remedies* have established themselves as invaluable sources of information and practical advice on the use of traditional Indian medicine.

Designed for easy reference and acoompanied by an extensive bibliography that notes existing scientific research on the medicinal qualities of various herbs, *Home Remedies* is an indispensible guide to good health for both the lay person and the practitioner of traditional medicine.

The Roots of Ayurveda

Edited and translated by Dominik Wujastyk

This volume brings together selections from the Sanskrit classics of the Ayurveda physicians Caraka, Susruta, Kasyapa, Vagabhata and Sarnagadhara who lived between mid-first millennium and the fourteenth century AD.

The constituents and systems of the physical body; the purifying nature of garlic therapy; the varieties of Soma juice and how they help rejuvenation; the dangers to kings from a variety of poisons including that of the snake maiden; rhinoplasty and other kinds of surgical operations; the circumstances leading to the loss of an embryo—these are among the subjects of esoteric and common interest which are described in detail here.

The translations, which are from the oldest extant writings of the physicians rather than from later commentaries, are in standard modern English. But care has been taken not to transpose English medical terms onto the Ayurvedic concepts. Dominik Wujastyk's authentic, critical and reader-friendly renderings of original Sanskrit medical texts offer us a glimpse into Ayurveda as a complete, scientific and living medical tradition.

You Can Do It!

Paul Hanna

In *You Can Do It!* Paul Hanna shows you how to take control of your life and guides you in the direction of greater success and happiness.

In this inspiring book you will discover:
- How to set goals and focus on them
- How to boost your self-confidence
- How winners come back from defeat
- How to improve your kid's self-esteem
- How to deal with negative people
- How to maintain your momentum
- How to avoid plateauing out
- How to recharge your marriage
- How to attract the good things in life
- How to use your time off as a tool for success

Calm at Work

Paul Wilson

If you have ever felt under pressure from the daily grind, this is the book for you. Paul Wilson, the author of *Instant Calm*, offers page after page of simple techniques to add calm, overcome stress and help get what you want from your work. You'll get through the work day feeling relaxed, positive and filfilled—and able to place work in the context of everything else in your life.

'Plenty of new-age gurus claim they have the answer to a stress-free life ... but when the word comes from a 45-year-old [businessman] who hustles each day in the tension-packed [business] world, the advice somehow has more credibility.'

—*New Woman*

'The guru of calm ...'

—*Sunday Times*

New Man for the New Millennium

Osho

In *New Man for the New Millennium*, Osho tells us why it is imperative that we become new human beings as we enter the new millennium. Osho says that only a new consciousness can deliver man from his bondage. He explains how this new consciousness can come only through us, from within ourselves. He shows us how to let go of the past, to go beyond ancient beliefs and to trust only in our experiences.

Osho elucidates the seven essential qualities of Homo Novus, the New Man. He takes a new look at issues that have eternally bedevilled generations: love and relationships, marriage and family, money, power, politics, work, and morality. He examines the challenges and opportunities of education, science and technology, the generation gap, government and the quality of life itself. For Osho, change, moving forward, and religion as a revolution is the way. And here he invites us to wake up to our enlightenment and revel and rejoice in life.